The

Light

Revolution

Richard Hobday

FINDHORN
Press

First published by Findhorn Press 2006 (UK) / 2007 (USA)

10054702 17

ISBN10: 1-84409-087-6
ISBN13: 978-1-84409-087-7

Edited by Jane Engel
Cover design by Damian Keenan
Interior design by Pam Bochel

Printed and bound by WS Bookwell, Finland

1 2 3 4 5 6 7 8 9 10 11 12 13 12 11 10 09 08 07 06

Published by
Findhorn Press
305A The Park, Findhorn, Forres
Scotland IV36 3TE
Tel 01309-690582 • Fax 01309-690036
eMail: info@findhornpress.com
www.findhornpress.com

Dedication

This book is dedicated to Mag and Harry
for their patience, understanding and support.

Disclaimer

The Light Revolution is intended to provide information on the beneficial effects of light. The advice given in the following pages has been compiled to this end, but it is not intended as a substitute for professional care. The author and publisher cannot accept any responsibility for ill-effects of exposure to ultraviolet radiation, to light, or any of the therapies described herein.

By the same author

The Healing Sun: Sunlight and Health in the 21st Century. Findhorn Press.

Sonnen Ohne Schattenseiten. VAK Concept.

Table of Contents

Acknowledgements

A large number of people influenced the contents of this book. Chief amongst them is my agent Caroline Davidson, of the Caroline Davidson and Literary Agency, without whose encouragement and expertise it would not have been accomplished. I also owe a great debt to John Palmer for his detailed comments on the manuscript. As ever, his rigour and critical abilities were invaluable. I am also indebted to my brother, John, for his technical and moral support.

The views expressed in the following pages are those of the author and do not necessarily reflect those of the experts who very kindly shared their knowledge with me. I am most grateful to the following: Professor Brian Norton, President of the Dublin Institute of Technology; Dr, Timo Partonen, National Public Health Institute, Helsinki, Finland; Professor Colin Porteous of the Mackintosh School of Architecture, Glasgow; Alex Attewell, Curator of the Florence Nightingale Museum, London; Dr. John Cason, King's College Hospital, London; Professor Marcus Newborough of Heriot Watt University, Edinburgh; Professor Jeffrey Stein, Department of Architecture, Wentworth Institute of Technology, Boston, Massachusetts; Professor Gary Baverstock, Research Institute for Sustainable Energy, Murdoch University, Perth, Australia; Dr. John Mardaljevic of the Institute of Energy and Sustainable Development, De Montfort University, Leicester; Jonathon David of the Chartered Institute of Building Services Engineers, London; Professor Clive Beggs of the School of Engineering Design and Technology, University of Bradford; Dr. Robert Lucas, School of Biological Sciences, University of Manchester; Dr. Barbara Boucher, Centre for Diabetes and Metabolic Medicine, Queen Mary School of Medicine and Dentistry, London; Dr. John J. Cannell, of The Vitamin D Council, Atascadero, California; Dr. William B. Grant of the Sunlight Nutrition and Health Research Center, San Francisco, California; Professor Eliyahu Ne'eman, Tel Aviv, Israel; Isabelle Godineau, Fondation Le Corbusier; Dion Neutra, the Neutra Institute for Survival Through Design, Los Angeles, California; Laura Bayliss of BDP Lighting, Manchester; Steven Hayes of Outside In, Cambridge; and Harry Miskin of the Caroline Davidson Literary Agency.

I must mention others who generously provided support and information: Graham Phillips; Dr. Robert Eli; Dr Joseph Mercola, Peter Hyde; Peter Carter; Simon Best; Margaret Campbell; Tim Welch; Frances

Penwarden; Bill Thayer, who assisted greatly with the classical references; Ray Munns, for the cartography; Marianne Crisp for the typing and, last but not least, Peter and Colette Davies.

For the reader who wishes to examine the evidence or do further research there is a bibliography, which includes all of the relevant sources. I would like to extend my thanks to the authors and researchers whose work I have referred to. I trust they will accept a citation of their work in lieu of an acknowledgement. Despite the best efforts of my publisher, Thierry Bogliolo, and his team at the Findhorn Press, and those of Pam Bochel and my editor Jane Engel, there are bound to be some errors and omissions in this book. They are entirely my own.

I wish particularly to thank Phoebe Harkins and her colleagues at the Wellcome Library for the History and Understanding of Medicine for the research they carried out on my behalf, together with the staff of the following libraries: the British Library; the RIBA Library; the Barnes Medical Library at the University of Birmingham; Birmingham Central Library; Aston University Library; Midhurst Public Library; Cwmbran Public Library; and the Library at the Welsh School of Architecture, Cardiff. I would also like to thank Caroline Tonson-Rye, the assistant editor of *Medical History* for her help with my article 'Sunlight therapy and solar architecture' of October 1997, some of which appears in Chapter 7 of this book. Also, some of the text in Chapter 4 was originally published in *Positive Health,* Issue 81 October 2002 (www.positivehealth.com) and appears courtesy of the editor, Dr. Sandra Goodman.

I hope that I have traced sources of all of the text and pictures still under copyright. However, should there be any acknowledgement referenced incorrectly, or inadvertently overlooked, the error will be rectified in subsequent editions by the Findhorn Press Ltd.

I would like to thank the following for their permission to reproduce selected copyright material:

The Architects' Journal for the drawing of E. Maxwell Fry's Sun House which appeared in the AJ on August 13th, 1936.

The British Medical Journal for the excerpt from 'The share of the sun in the prevention and treatment of tuberculosis' by Dr. A. Rollier which appeared in the BMJ on October 21st 1922.

The Batsford Press for the excerpt from *Environment and Services* by Peter Burberry, 1977.

Dover Publications Inc., New York, for *The Ten Books on Architecture* by Vitruvius. (trans. M. Hickey Morgan) 1960.

Faber and Faber for the excerpt from *Fine Building* by E. Maxwell Fry, 1944.

Her Majesty's Stationery Office, London, for the excerpt from the House of Commons Health Committee Report on Obesity. Third Report of Session 2003–04, Volume I,London, HMSO 2004.

Penguin Books for excerpts from *Pliny The Elder: Natural History – A Selection* (Trans. J. F. Healey) 1991, and *Seneca: Letters from a Stoic* (Trans. R. A. Campbell), 1975.

The map of Pompeii is reproduced courtesy of Current World Archaeology (www.archaeology.co.uk)

Photographic Credits

The photograph of George Bernard Shaw is reproduced courtesy of the EMPICS photographic agency.

The photograph of rickets is reproduced courtesy of the Wellcome Library, London.

List of Figures

Introduction

Nearly five thousand years ago work began on Egypt's first pyramid; the Step Pyramid at Saqqara, near Memphis. The architect in charge was a supremely gifted man, who was also a doctor, an astronomer and the high priest of an Egyptian solar cult. Today, Imhotep is remembered as the master-builder of one of the world's great monuments; but he also represents something fundamental to our health. Imhotep personifies the historic link between the sun, architecture and medicine.

Sunlit buildings save lives. This is no idle claim. The evidence is there. Patients in hospital wards suffer less pain and are less likely to catch infections if they can see the sun. Heart attack victims stand a better chance of recovery if they are in sunlit rooms. Depressed psychiatric patients fare better if they get some sun while in hospital, as do premature babies with jaundice. We all benefit from being in a sunlit environment to some degree. Unfortunately, our buildings, our streets and our cities are not as sympathetic to sunlight as they might be; and a great deal that should have been practised continuously since Imhotep's time has not been. Lessons have been relearned and techniques reinvented, only to be forgotten again. The chapters in this book explain why this happened, and what it means for our health both in and outside buildings. This is not an easy journey. Nevertheless, it is a journey worth taking.

Throughout history, writers and artists have drawn their inspiration from the sun. Luminaries such as Homer, Plato, Pliny, William Shakespeare, John Donne, J.M.W. Turner, Percy Shelley and Vincent Van Gogh have each, in their own unique way, paid homage to the sun in their work. Some of them recognised that it stimulated and enhanced their creative powers and none more so than the great Irish dramatist George Bernard Shaw who wrote many of his most famous plays in a small shed in the garden of his Hertfordshire home. So important was sunlight to George Bernard Shaw that he had his shed on a turntable and could adjust its position to follow the path of the sun.

My own interest in the benefits of living and working in sunlit spaces was less elevated. During the 1980s I was one of a team of engineers and scientists who were trying to find out whether buildings that admit direct sunlight use less energy than those that do not. The results of our research were favourable: they showed that well-designed solar dwellings typically use about 25 to 50 per cent less heating and lighting energy than comparable non-solar buildings. Also, when we interviewed the occupants to get their views on the merits, or otherwise, of solar architecture, they all said that they valued living and working in sunlit spaces. Many said that they wouldn't wish to return to a conventional building because they would miss the sun. Intrigued by this, I went through all the relevant publications on architecture and building design in the mistaken belief there would be a lot of information on the positive effect of sunlight. Yet there was little modern evidence to support the idea that sunlit buildings were in any way healthier than dwellings that excluded the sun's rays. Seemingly, sunlight was low on the list of things to consider when planning a building. Indeed, it barely made it on to the list at all. Then, while turning the pages of an engineering textbook, *Environment and Services*, I found out why:

> *Until recently the health-giving properties of the sun's rays were thought important but medical opinion has changed considerably on this issue and in addition the germicidal effects of sunshine in interiors are not now considered significant in relation to modern cleaning methods.*

Sunlight has been used as a medicine for thousands of years. The *Ebers Papyrus,* one of the oldest surviving Egyptian medical texts, recommends exposure to the sun. Some of the most distinguished figures in Greek, Roman and Islamic medicine used sunlight to prevent and cure disease. In 1903, just over one hundred years ago, the Nobel Prize for Medicine was awarded to Niels Finsen, a Danish doctor who put sunlight therapy at the forefront of medicine after centuries of neglect. In the years that followed, hospitals and sanatoriums were built so that patients with tuberculosis and rickets could be exposed to the sun under medical supervision. During the First World War, military surgeons used sunlight to disinfect and heal wounds, and until about 50 years ago, medical experts promoted sunbathing. Doctors knew sunlight speeded up the healing process. But there was no scientific basis for the 'sun-cure' or heliotherapy, as it became known. Nor were there any scientific theories to explain why patients recovered more quickly in sunlit wards than dark wards; but they did.

By the 1970s, when the textbook I referred to was written, the tide was turning against the sun. The war against germs had finally been won – antibiotics had seen to that – or so everyone thought. Rickets and tuberculosis were vanquished and there was no longer any need to get sunlight into hospitals to kill bacteria. Soon governments around the world were running concerted public relations campaigns to raise public awareness of the dangers of sunbathing. Any notion that the sun's rays could be beneficial, either outdoors, or inside buildings, was dispelled and so architects stopped designing for them.

Ironically, medical experts began to stigmatise the sun just as the health effects of bright artificial light gained recognition. During the 1980s evidence emerged of a link between depressive illness and light deprivation. Based on this and other more recent findings, it has become clear that building occupants do not get enough bright light to have a positive impact on their health. The light levels required for this are much higher than those needed to perform visual tasks. Electric lighting developed under the assumption that the only significant purpose of light for humans is to see. Until recently the impact of artificial light on physiological and psychological well-being was not considered.

As buildings are no longer designed for the sun, opportunities to benefit from light of sufficient intensity to have a favourable impact on our health can be limited in the modern world. This may explain why depression is becoming so common. According to the World Health Organization, depressive disorders are the fourth leading cause of ill-health among adults worldwide, and by the year 2020 severe depression will be second only to cardiovascular disease as the main cause of death and disability. Meanwhile, some of the bacteria that antibiotics were supposed to have dealt with 30 years ago are now untreatable.

One of the so-called 'superbugs' that infect our hospitals is becoming established in the wider community. The MRSA bacterium, or methicillin-resistant *Staphylococcus aureus*, has long been a serious problem in wards and nursing homes where it infects patients weakened by disease or injury. But a strain has emerged that can infect healthy young people who have had no prior hospital exposure. With drug-resistant bacteria posing an ever-greater threat to public health, sunlight's germicidal properties may soon be more of a priority for designers than they have been.

Then there is the problem of vitamin D deficiency. This is now so common among the general public that it is referred to as an 'unrecognised epidemic.' Large sections of the population are unaware that unless they expose themselves to the sun at regular intervals they will have very low levels of vitamin D in their bodies. This places them at risk of a range of common conditions such as heart disease, stroke, hypertension, depression, diabetes, cancer, hip fractures and osteoporosis. The latest findings on vitamin D, those on resistant bacteria, and those on the human body's response to bright light, suggest that George Bernard Shaw was right to turn his hut towards the sun after all.

Of course, Shaw was not the first person to appreciate sunlight and to change his position relative to it. Florence Nightingale was equally enthusiastic, as she explained in her famous *Notes on Nursing*, which were published in 1860:

> It is the unqualified result of all my experience with the sick, that second only to their need of fresh air is their need of light; that, after a close room, what hurts them most is a dark room. And it is not only light but direct sun-light that they want. I had rather have the power of carrying my patient about after the sun, according to the aspect of the rooms, if the circumstances permit, than let him linger in a room when the sun is off. People think that the effect is on the spirits only. This is by no means the case. The sun is not only a painter but a sculptor.

Florence Nightingale made these observations when, as now, architects and doctors were largely unaware of the health benefits of getting sunlight indoors. Miss Nightingale was the driving force behind the construction of some of the first sunlit hospital wards of the modern era. Her thinking on the subject was in advance of scientific opinion and ran counter to the prevailing orthodoxy which was to keep patients in the dark. It took 50 years for her ideas to gain acceptance. Today they are largely ignored. Yet the latest research supports many of Miss Nightingale's assertions about the positive impact of sunlight on the recovery of hospital patients, and has profound implications for our health inside and outside buildings.

Much that was once known about sunlight therapy and lighting buildings for health has been overlooked, or forgotten. By the time that electric lighting became cheap and efficient, medical science had abandoned the ancient notion that light, darkness, and the change of seasons could influence disease. Natural light ceased to be the daytime illuminant of choice, and the skills required to use it for health were not passed on. Also, today knowledge does not move from one discipline to another as readily as it used to. Skills are not shared. Gone are the days when architects knew about medicine or doctors knew how to design hospitals.

In my previous book *The Healing Sun* I discussed some of the benefits of sun exposure and explained how doctors practised heliotherapy. *The Light Revolution* brings together historical evidence, traditional wisdom and the latest scientific findings to show why buildings that let in sunlight can be far healthier than those that do not. It also explains how, and why, some of the 20th century's greatest architects designed for the sun.

Chapter 1
Nothing New under the Sun

Recent discoveries about light and health are going to change the way we live and work. They confirm what has long been suspected: that light has a profound effect both on our immune systems and our emotional stability; and that lighting for vision only is not enough. Indeed, it may be harmful. Architects and physicians in the ancient world and in more recent times knew this. Or, at least, they recognised that the light levels needed to promote well-being were much higher than those required for vision – which are the ones typically used in modern indoor environments. We need to start doing what they did and illuminate for health, which means more light during the day and more darkness at night. The conventional approach to lighting buildings is effectively obsolete.

Although research into indoor light and our well-being is in its infancy, there is now more than enough evidence to justify the claim that a revolution is upon us. In 2002, scientists found something that places a premium on light, especially in buildings. They reported in the journal *Science* that they had discovered a new sensory system in the human eye. This is not involved in vision: it is there to receive and respond to light, sending signals directly to the body's biological clock. This clock, in turn, regulates the secretion of hormones and neurotransmitters in the brain, including melatonin and serotonin. These have a direct influence on our health and the amount of light and darkness we expose ourselves to dictates when, and how much of them, is secreted.

Although bright light is known to have health benefits, and has been used to treat conditions such as seasonal affective disorder (SAD) and non-seasonal depression for some time, no one knows exactly how, or why, it works. But discovery of this new photosensitive system explains a great deal about the ways in which light affects our well-being. And it supports the age-old belief that we need to be able to see bright light to stay healthy.

Coincidentally, in 2002 scientists made another discovery about light and health: they published results in the *The Lancet* which showed there is a link between sunlight, serotonin and, by implication, depression.

They found that levels of this neurotransmitter in the brain are lowest during the autumn and winter and highest in spring and summer, when sunlight is most plentiful. They also found that the rate of production of serotonin by the brain was directly related to the duration of sunlight and rose rapidly as the sun grew brighter. If, as it seems, the secretion of serotonin in our brains is governed by the amount of sunlight that is available to us, this is an important finding because our serotonin levels can determine how cheerful or depressed we are.

Another significant breakthrough came in April 2005, when a study published in the *American Journal of Psychiatry* concluded that light therapy is as effective as medication in the treatment of major depressive illnesses and that it has fewer side effects. Exactly why bright light so effectively reduces the symptoms of this common condition is still something of a mystery. But it points to an underlying biological cause for depression, and helps to dispel some of the scepticism that persists about the influence of light on this and other mental illnesses. These findings should change the way psychiatrists treat depression, and the way in which buildings are illuminated.

Much remains to be discovered about the mechanisms through which bright light exerts its beneficial effects. What is clear is that few of us get enough light during the day to have a positive impact on our minds and bodies. Perpetual twilight is not what nature intended for us yet we now spend, on average, about 90 per cent of our time indoors and much of this is at low light levels.

History has a habit of repeating itself and, as George Bernard Shaw noted, people do not learn as much from the lessons it has to offer as they might. This is as true of medicine and architecture as any other field of human endeavour. Take, for example, the idea that lethargy, sadness and despair can be brought on by light deprivation. Physicians in ancient Greece and Rome accurately described much of what is now known about mood disorders. They called the emotion associated with gloom and darkness 'melancholia',

Fig. 1. Mr. George Bernard Shaw turning his shed to catch the sun's rays

and during the second century AD the Greek doctor Aretaeus of Cappadocia presented western medicine with the first complete portrayal of depressive illness. Significantly, he wrote of it that:

> Lethargics are to be laid out in the light and exposed to the
> rays of the sun, for the disease is gloom.

Note the direct and unambiguous reference to the sun's rays. Few doctors would be prepared to be so forthright about the benefits of sunlight in today's climate. Aretaeus had the good fortune to practise medicine in Rome when architects were building for the sun. Under Roman law there were rights to the sun. During the third century AD Ulpian, a Roman jurist and imperial official, decreed that for most purposes it was enough just to have a right-to-light. But in two specific cases, that of the solarium and the 'heliocaminus,' there was a right to direct sunlight. The Romans covered their window spaces with mica or glass and referred to a room that trapped direct sunlight as a heliocaminus, or sun furnace. Sun-right laws ensured the Romans could heat their buildings economically and keep themselves healthy. Rome's public baths let in the sun to keep fuel costs down and provided citizens with facilities for sunbathing, as the statesman and philosopher Seneca (4BC–65AD) described in his correspondence:

> Nowadays 'moth-hole' is the way some people speak of a
> bathroom unless it has been designed to catch the sun
> through enormous windows all day long, unless a person can
> acquire a tan at the same time as he is having a bath, unless
> he has views from the bath over the countryside and sea.

Doctors of the period wrote of the benefits of sun exposure and Roman architecture reflects this. Indeed, sunlight was so important to the Romans that by the third century AD sun worship had become the state religion. Also, the Romans were more concerned with preventing disease than in finding cures for ailments, which is why they attached so much importance to hygiene and sanitation and why they invested so heavily in public health measures. Protecting the ordinary citizen and the army from disease was a priority. The Roman statesman Marcus Tullius Cicero (106–43BC) famously wrote that 'The health of the people is the highest law.' Presumably, this is why they built so many aqueducts, sewers, public baths and lavatories, and why they came to value the sun so highly.

Whenever Rome's legions occupied new territory they used their considerable engineering skills to overcome and then subdue the indigenous population. The Romans mastered the art of bridge building, which meant that their troops and supplies could cross rivers rapidly in all weathers. The Romans also imposed themselves on the landscape by building new towns away from existing settlements, and by linking them with durable, obsessively straight roads. And they introduced sanitation, clean water, baths, amphitheatres and imposing public monuments wherever they went. As Pliny the Elder (AD 23–79) remarked:

> *...we have conquered the world with our buildings too.*

Engineers enjoyed much influence in Rome's affairs both at home and abroad. Doctors, such as Areteaus, did not enjoy the same status. Medicine was an occupation unworthy of the Roman citizen, being the trade of slaves, freedmen and foreigners. The author Pliny the Elder had little time for the medical fraternity. In his encyclopaedia *Natural History* he explains that the Romans relied instead on hygiene and the sun. They had managed for 600 years without doctors and were wise to do so. In his opinion doctors were untrustworthy, greedy and, above all, dangerous:

> *Doctors learn by exposing us to risks, and conduct experiments*
> *at the expense of our lives. Only a doctor can kill with*
> *impunity.*

Pliny had a higher regard for the main sewer that ran beneath the Eternal City than any doctor. Of course, Pliny's is a rather partial view. Some doctors achieved positions of prestige and influence in Roman society, while others were popular with the ordinary citizen. But the sentiments that Pliny expressed are not unique: George Bernard Shaw made similar observations in the Introduction of his play *The Doctor's Dilemma* in which he also, like Pliny, discussed the importance of sunlight to health. And both men were enthusiastic sunbathers. Archaeological excavations at Herculanium, in southern Italy, provide evidence that a solarium was an important part of the winter residence of the Roman upper class. We also know from the writings of the military engineer and architect Vitruvius (fl. 46–30 BC) that the Roman's best villas, baths and health temples were carefully orientated for the sun.

While Rome's sanitary arrangements serve as a model for all that has been done in public health since, the citizens of Rome enjoyed one benefit we do not: their right to sunlight. When the legions withdrew from Britain at the beginning of the 5th century they took their engineering know-how and sun-rights with them. Little is known about the medical use of light in the years that followed. There is barely a reference to it in western medical literature from the Fall of Rome to the end of the 17th century. For much of this time sunbathing seems to have been regarded as a pagan practice synonymous with sun-worship, while doctors and architects attached rather less importance to light, hygiene and sanitation than the Romans had.

By the 1840s the idea of public health re-emerged in Britain in response to the squalor, and misery of life in the new industrial towns. Florence Nightingale discovered the benefits of sun exposure and began insisting on sunlight in her hospital wards. As she wrote in her *Notes on Hospitals* in 1859:

> *Direct sunlight, not only daylight, is necessary for speedy recovery.*

Towards the end of the 19th century scientists began to investigate the therapeutic and sanitary properties of the sun's rays and these came to be more widely recognised. The bactericidal properties of sunlight were discovered by Dr. Arthur Downes and Mr. Thomas Blunt, who reported their findings to the Royal Society in 1877. In 1903, Niels Finsen was awarded the Nobel Prize for Physiology in recognition of his success in treating tuberculosis with concentrated ultra-violet light. Finsen's cure for tuberculosis was adopted by physicians in a number of countries and stimulated great interest in the healing powers of the sun. In the same year, 1903, Dr. Auguste Rollier began to use sunlight to treat tuberculosis and rickets at his Alpine clinic in Switzerland; these diseases were commonplace in the polluted industrial cities of Europe and the United States.

The renewed appreciation of the sanitary and therapeutic properties of sunlight brought about by the work of Finsen, Rollier and others had a marked effect on building design from the turn of the 20th century onwards. Architects produced buildings that were well sunlit to promote health and hygiene, and none more so than the pioneers of modern architecture. In his influential manifesto *The Athens Charter,* Le Corbusier proclaimed that to bring in the sun was the new and the most imperative duty of the architect. But there was nothing new about it. On the contrary, architects had been doing it for millennia, but only when the sun's rays were thought to be beneficial. Unfortunately, when the sun falls from grace with the medical establishment, as it has on numerous occasions, there is little reason for architects to make provision for it. So they do not, unless fuel for heating is in very short supply.

Modern research does confirm much of what Miss Nightingale and others from the past believed about lighting buildings. It is becoming clear that there is a range of non-visual, systemic effects of light in humans. The latest findings give us a much better understanding of them. In doing so, they highlight a great failing of both the medical and building professions: a reluctance to embrace their respective histories as warmly as they might. Indeed, at times they display an almost Maoist contempt for the past. The link between light deprivation and depressive illness, which Aretaeus of Cappadocia so clearly identified nearly 2,000 years ago was scientifically proven as recently as in the 1980's. The observations of Aretaeus on the positive impact of direct sunlight on depression continue to be largely overlooked, as does the positive influence of sunlight on another psychological condition, that of pain.

Sun and Pain Perception

In 2005, a study in the journal *Psychosomatic Medicine* showed that sunlight in a hospital room affects both the pain level patients feel and the amount of analgesic medication they need to cope with it. A group of patients recovering from spinal fusion surgery did so in wards that were either on the 'bright' or the 'dim' side of a unit at Montefiore University Hospital in Pittsburgh. Those in the bright rooms received an average of 46 per cent more sunlight each day than equally ill patients assigned to darker rooms. Patients who had greater sun exposure reported that they experienced less stress and less pain both immediately after surgery and on discharge from hospital. And they needed 22 per cent less medication each hour to control their pain following surgery. Sunlight produced its greatest analgesic effect on the first day after surgery. Patients in the most pain were the ones who received the most benefit from sunlight exposure. The drugs used to relieve pain in postoperative patients have side effects that include nausea, vomiting, urinary problems and constipation. The incidence of side effects increases with the dose. And these drugs are expensive. The patients on the bright side had an average of 21 per cent reduction in analgesic medication cost compared with patients on the dim side.

The press heralded these results as the first evidence that sunlight could influence the perception of pain. However, it is clear from the *Ebers Papyrus*, which dates from around 1550 BC, that the ancients were familiar with the concept:

> To relieve any painful part... the body is anointed and exposed
> to the sun.

Then again, during the First World War, when military surgeons routinely put infected gunshot and shrapnel wounds out in the sun to disinfect them, they found the same thing. One of their number, the Swiss surgeon and sunlight therapist Dr. Oskar Bernhard (1861–1939), wrote in his book *Light Treatment in Surgery* that:

> ...the remarkable analgesic effect of the sun's rays, has as yet received no physiological explanation... The reduction of pain, which insolation soon brings about, even in deep-seated diseases, may probably be connected with the process of healing.

The first scientific evidence that pain plays an important role in wound healing appeared in 2006, in a study published in the *Annals of Behavioural Medicine.* This showed the more pain patients feel following a surgical procedure the longer they take to recover. Stress from pain, or any other source, produces hormones in the body that slow the rate at which wounds heal and a decrease in the functioning of the immune system. This, in turn, increases susceptibility to wound infections. People feel less pain if they are in a good mood and under less stress. Research shows that bright light improves negative mood states and that sunlight triggers the release of 'feel-good' brain chemicals such as serotonin and endorphins. Serotonin acts as a pain inhibitor in the spinal chord and other areas of the central nervous system. There may be other as yet unidentified processes at work, but the relief of pain does influence healing. And, as Dr. Bernhard identified 70 years ago, and the Egyptians before him, sunlight is a painkiller.

Based on historical and present-day evidence, if hospital wards were arranged for the sun, patients would be spared unnecessary suffering and delay in recovery. In addition, hospital pharmacy costs would be significantly reduced and patients would experience fewer drug-related side effects and drug-to-drug interactions.

Sunlight and Jaundice

Another medical condition that responds favourably to sunlight is jaundice, which is common in babies; especially those born prematurely. One of the first doctors to advocate sun exposure for jaundice, Soranus of Ephesus, did so in about 100 AD. Soranus was one of Imperial Rome's more distinguished physicians. He was a paediatrician, a gynaecologist and the author of several medical texts. Unfortunately, in a similar manner to Aretaeus, Soranus' ideas about sunlight and jaundice were overlooked for more than a thousand years. It was not until 1956 that the benefits of putting jaundiced babies out in the sun were rediscovered by Sister Janice Ward, a nurse in charge of a premature baby unit at the Rochford Hospital, Essex, in England.

Since then the standard treatment for jaundice in babies has been to put them under 'bili lamps' rather than out in the sun. These lamps are so-called because the blue light they emit is effective in breaking down a substance called bilirubin in the blood of jaundiced babies. Bilirubin is normally removed by the liver and, before birth, the mother's liver does this for the baby. However, following birth, it can take a few days for babies' livers to start removing bilirubin effectively, and their skin and the whites of their eyes can take on a yellow hue. In most infants this is harmless, but sometimes the bilirubin level can be high enough to cause brain damage.

Clearly, sunlight has a direct influence on liver metabolism. So far, there is only one study that shows that this applies indoors as well as outside. An article in the *British Medical Journal* in 1985 described an epidemic of jaundice in an obstetric ward following a reduction in sunlight levels. The ward had been brightly lit, and the incidence of jaundice low, but then the roof overhangs above the ward's windows were extended, cutting out the sun and increasing the incidence of jaundice.

Planning for the Sun

From these and other studies it is clear that limiting peoples' access to sunlight can make them very ill indeed. Access to the sun is vitally important, yet the manner in which buildings are now designed (and towns and cities are planned) pays little regard to this. For example, in Arab countries the traditional open courtyard-type house used to give women a private setting in which they could remove the veil and the long-sleeved clothing they wear in public. They could chat, play with their children, prepare food, do the washing and receive enough sunlight exposure to synthesise vitamin D. Replacement of these traditional-style houses with smaller modern houses, apartment blocks or skyscrapers may have damaged their health considerably. Vitamin D deficiency is now common among Arab women and children even though they live in some of the sunniest countries in the world.

The layout of cities can also decide the vitamin D status of the people who inhabit them. Tall buildings block out the sun. Planners who allow them to be built, or who encourage the use of automotive transport rather than travel by foot or bicycle, limit opportunities for vitamin D synthesis. This is a subject we will return to later, but for the moment let us look at the ways in which the education of an architect can influence such matters.

Two thousand years ago, in a less technical age, the skills of the architect had to be broader than they are today. In Roman times the architect was, from the word's Greek etymology, a 'chief technician' who was responsible for directing the work of specialized craftsman. The main difference between then and now is that antiquity did not recognise the 19th century distinction between architecture and mechanical engineering. This is obvious when one reads the only comprehensive essay on ancient building that posterity has passed down to us, the *Ten Books on Architecture*. Written in the 1st century BC, by a retired military engineer named Marcus Vitruvius Pollio, the *Ten Books* cover aqueducts, pumps, clocks, cranes, site planning, public health, solar design, artillery, and siege engines. The *Ten Books* are dedicated to the Emperor – probably Vitruvius' former employer Augustus Caesar. Vitruvius compiled them because he wanted Rome's extensive public building programme to be a success. He drew Caesar's attention to what he saw as a lack of professionalism among other architects. To do the job properly architects had to be widely educated in the arts and sciences, and be knowledgeable about medicine too:

> ...on account of the question of climates, air, the healthiness
> and unhealthiness of sites, and the use of different waters. For
> without these considerations, the healthiness of a dwelling
> cannot be assured.

A valid point, given Rome's commitment to the well-being of its citizens. Astronomy was another subject in the Vitruvian syllabus. The true architect designed for sunlight, and a prerequisite for this was an intimate knowledge of the sun's path through the heavens. Cities and temples had to be orientated without the aid of a magnetic compass in those days and so directions had to be worked out from the position of the sun and stars. Vitruvius devoted one of his ten books to the subject of astronomy, even including detailed instructions on mounting and calibrating sundials.

Now we know from genetics and neuroscience that our brains are identical to those of our ancestors. Our response to sunlight is the same as the ancient Egyptians when they were laying the foundations of the Step Pyramid, or that of the Romans when they were sunbathing at their public baths. But when Thomas Edison patented the electric light bulb just over 100 years ago he changed our relationship with the sun. Edison's invention ushered in a 24-hour society where light is available at the flick of a switch. Gradually we became separated, if not entirely divorced, from the sun's daily and seasonal cycles. We don't need the sun to light our buildings, nor do we worship the sun, and for the last 20 years we've been told to stay out of sunlight because it is dangerous. So, perhaps it might be useful to remind ourselves just how much significance the sun held for the Romans, and not just in their architecture, or as a medicine, or an energy source. The author and polymath Pliny the Elder wrote in his encyclopaedia *Natural History* that the sun was nothing less than the supreme deity hidden behind the numerous lesser gods of Greece and Rome:

> *When we consider his functions we must believe that the sun is the soul, or, more intelligibly, the mind of the universe, the ruling principle and divinity of Nature. The sun provides the world with light and takes away darkness: he blacks out and lights up the rest of the stars. The sun controls the change of the seasons and the continual regeneration of the year, following Nature's practice. He dispels the gloomy aspect of heaven and lightens the clouds over men's minds. He lends his light to the rest of the stars, is splendid, supreme and sees and hears everything; I observe that Homer, the most distinguished person in the field of literature, held this view about the sun's function.*

Beliefs such as these informed the architecture of Rome just as they had that of Greece and before that Egypt. Back then it was the architect's job to build in harmony with the sun. Today, thanks to technological advances and decades of cheap energy, architects are not obliged to. Nor do they have the medical knowledge that Vitruvius insisted on. The Romans built to prevent disease and, while they were not too keen on doctors, their engineers and architects clearly learned from them. In marked contrast, health is not such a priority for present-day designers. They attach more importance to energy conservation and broader environmental concerns than to the physical, psychological and emotional demands they place on the occupants of their buildings. The building professions have largely abandoned what was once one of their most important functions: designing to promote well-being. Predictably others have stepped in to fill the vacuum. The way in which the ancient

Chinese art of Feng Shui has become popular with homeowners and leading figures in the business community in recent years illustrates the point. Medicine does not feature in the modern architect's syllabus, nor does solar design of the type practised by Vitruvius and his contemporaries. If it did we might be spared some of the worst effects of light deprivation. But then modern medicine, like architecture, attaches rather less importance to sunlight than it did in the past.

Chapter 2
Light and Health

All life on earth takes its cue from the sun. Waking and sleeping, fertility and growth, migration and hibernation are some of the many natural cycles that are driven by the sun's waxing and waning. Our ancestors knew it was in their interests to live in harmony with the sun. By contrast, over the last 50 years the human race has done what it can to try and exist independently of daily and seasonal changes in light levels. The sun has important messages for us but few of us get them because we spend so much time indoors. The latest research suggests that when the sun is out we should be outside too getting enough of its brightness to reset our biological clocks, and enough of its rays on our skin to build up our reserves of vitamin D. Then, when the sun disappears below the horizon, so should we. Or, at least, we should be seeking darkness and avoiding bright light if we want to stay healthy.

Before we begin to look at some of the many ways in which light influences us mentally and physically, imagine for a moment what daily life must have been like among a primitive tribe that lacked the skills needed to make fire. During the day there would be much hunting and gathering and an unrelieved diet of raw food. Nighttime would be cold and, on occasion, sleepless too because with no fire for protection, the going down of the sun meant that hunter-gatherers could easily fall victim to nocturnal predators. If this were not bad enough there was always the possibility that the sun might disappear altogether. To the ancients the sun was a sentient being with a mind of his, or her, own. When the sun fell below the horizon at dusk it might deign to reappear on the horizon the following morning. Then again, it might not. And as winter set in, and the nights became longer, there was no guarantee that they would shorten once the winter solstice – the shortest day – had passed. From the dawn of history our ancestors conducted ceremonies and rituals to propitiate the sun and try to ensure its return, or its rebirth. They raised stone circles, shrines and temples where they faced the sun during their devotions. And they oriented churches and cathedrals to the same end, though a little more discretely. Like our ancestors, we are programmed to respond to the sun. We are outdoor animals, attuned to the pronounced changes in light levels that occur between the sun's rising and setting.

Sunlight affects our minds and bodies differently according to the time of day and time of year. At this point it might be helpful to acquaint ourselves with the sun's apparent movement through the heavens, if only to find out what we may be missing. The traditional way of doing this is to place a vertical rod in the ground and watch the shadow it casts. The ancients erected stone pillars and obelisks, otherwise known as 'gnomons', for this. The triangular plate on top of a sundial serves the same purpose.

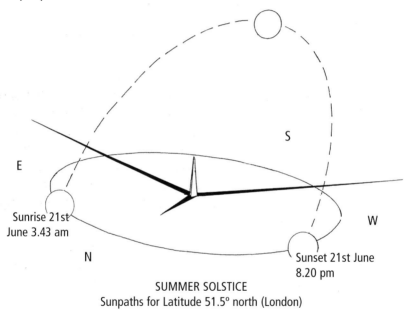

SUMMER SOLSTICE
Sunpaths for Latitude 51.5° north (London)

Fig. 2. Shadows cast by a Gnomon on the Summer Solstice

A shadow cast by a gnomon in the summer, when the noonday sun is almost overhead, will be much shorter than when the sun is lower in the sky later in the day. Figure 2 shows the shortest shadow of all which is thrown at midday on the summer solstice. This is the longest day of the year and occurs around the 21st of June.

When the shadow cast by a gnomon at noon is longest, as shown in Figure 3, this defines the winter solstice that falls around the 21st of December. Each day after the winter solstice, the sun's path becomes a little higher in the southern sky. The sun also begins to rise closer to the

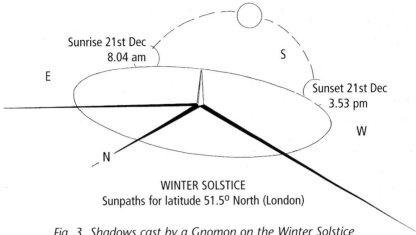

WINTER SOLSTICE
Sunpaths for latitude 51.5° North (London)

Fig. 3. Shadows cast by a Gnomon on the Winter Solstice

east and set closer to the west until the day eventually comes when it rises exactly east and sets exactly west, otherwise known as the spring equinox. To identify when the spring and autumn equinoxes occur our ancestors would have marked the ground where the shadows fall at sunrise and sunset on the 21st of March and 21st September, or thereabouts. If the marks from the two shadows formed a continuous line, as shown in Figure 4, it meant the sun had risen in the east and set exactly in the west. This signifies that day and night are of equal length, and thus defines the equinox.

The sun rises due east and sets due west on the equinoxes at all latitudes. The angle between the east-west equinox sunrise line and the solstice sunrises depends on the latitude of the observer. For example, at a latitude of 51° north, that of Stonehenge, on midsummer's day our ancestors would have seen the sun rise in the northeast and set in the northwest. On midwinter's day the sun rises in the southeast and sets in the southwest.

By making a few simple observations such as these one can develop an awareness of where the sun will be at any given time, and of how strong it is. For those of us who live a long way from the equator the four key points of the solar year point to changes in our environment, and in our minds and bodies too. None more so than the passing of the autumn equinox. This is an event that has implications for our health because it marks the onset of what doctors used to refer to as the period of 'vitamin D famine'. At this time of year in Britain the ultraviolet radiation in sunlight starts to fall below the threshold level at which we can synthesize

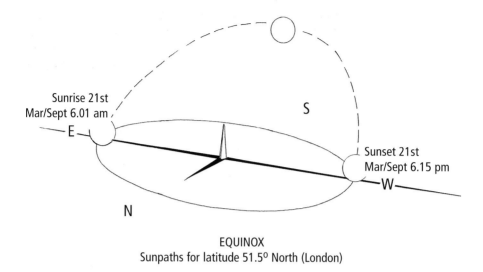

Sunrise 21st
Mar/Sept 6.01 am

E

S

Sunset 21st
Mar/Sept 6.15 pm

W

N

EQUINOX
Sunpaths for latitude 51.5° North (London)

Fig. 4. Shadows cast by a Gnomon on the Equinoxes

vitamin D in our skin. It remains below this level for six months, until the spring equinox has passed. Between the autumn and spring equinoxes we cannot rely on the sun for our supplies of vitamin D. We rely on the stores we have built up during the summer months, or what little vitamin D there is in our diets. By the middle of winter most of our reserves have gone.

Day length changes slowly around December 21st and June 21st – the shortest and longest days – and rapidly at the time of the equinoxes. The word solstice has its origins in the word *solstitium,* meaning 'the sun stands still.' So there are many long, light days in the summer and many short, dark ones in the winter. In other words, there are more days in the winter months that are like December 21st and more days in the summer like June 21st, than there are days like March 21st and September 21st.

The amount and intensity of light available to us daily and seasonally changes markedly; and much more so when outside than indoors. At noon in summer, for example, when the sun is at its highest point above the horizon, its illuminance is 100,000 lux, or more. Later in the day, when the sun is just above the horizon, its luminance falls to less than one-tenth of this: to about 8,200 lux. When the sun's disc first touches the horizon its illuminance is below 2,800 lux and when the centre of the sun is at the horizon we are down to 750 lux. This falls to just 500 lux once the sun's upper edge dips below the horizon. In marked contrast, lighting within buildings is more subdued: light levels in homes and offices are often between 50 and 500 lux. So most of us spend 90 per cent of our time indoors, in twilight; living as if the sun were permanently below the horizon. Here are some typical figures for different lighting regimes:

- moonlight: 0.5 lux

- a living room at night, in front of the TV: 15-50 lux

- the middle of a large office: 100 lux

- a well-lit kitchen or office: 500 lux

- a heavily overcast winter's day: 1,000 lux

- sitting next to a window: 1000–2000 lux

- a clear spring morning, about 30 minutes after sunrise: 10,000 lux

- phototherapy for SAD from a light box: 2,500–10,000 lux

- a sunny summer's day: 50,000–150,000 lux

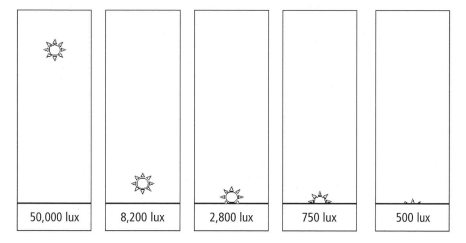

Fig. 5. Typical Solar Iluminances

Another way of looking at this is to add up the amount of light we get over the course of a day. Someone working indoors in 250 lux for 8 hours receives 2,000 lux hours of light. If the same person spent 8 hours outdoors at an average of 10,000 lux they would be exposed to 80,000 lux hours, or 40 times more light. In addition, when outdoors they would experience marked variations in light levels over the 8 hours in question, and they would see the spectral composition of the sun's rays vary too. Sunlight changes colour as the weather changes and as dust and moisture in the air increase and decrease. When the sun is low in the sky its rays have to pass through the ozone layer and the earth's atmosphere at an oblique angle. This results in greater absorption, scattering, and diffusion than when the sun is at its zenith, which is why there is so much red and yellow in the sky at sunrise and sunset. Sunlight is dynamic: think of a cloud passing across the sun; dappled shade; a shaft of sunlight breaking through trees; or a rainbow. Someone confined indoors would be largely unaware of many of the changes of colour and intensity that occur over a day unless they could see the sun through a window. But this would mean they were getting far more than 250 lux. They could be getting 50,000 lux, or more.

Does the fact that few of us in the modern industrialised world see much sunlight matter? Well, it seems reasonable to suggest that if hospital patients who are in pain, are jaundiced or are otherwise unwell benefit from seeing the sun, then there are good grounds for thinking that people who are healthy might benefit too. However, before enlarging on this it might be useful to define what we mean by sunlight and daylight. Sunlight is solar radiation that has reached the earth's surface as parallel rays. Daylight is a combination of sunlight and skylight, the latter being solar radiation that has reached the earth's surface after scattering in the atmosphere. Skylight comes from all directions, sunlight only one which is why it produces strong, clearly defined shadows. The proportion of skylight to sunlight is determined by the distance solar radiation travels through the atmosphere and how much water vapour it passes through on its way to us. It is this scattering by water vapour that gives the sky its blue appearance. Confusion sometimes arises because people often refer to daylight when, in fact, they mean skylight. This is an important distinction, not least in buildings.

Daylight or Skylight?

Designers calculate how much natural light there will be in a room as a percentage of the amount of skylight outdoors. They use what is known as the Daylight Factor, which has been the method of choice for the last 50 years or so. A Daylight Factor of 4 to 5 per cent is often specified in schoolrooms or other places where people are going to undertake demanding visual tasks. On this basis, if there's 10,000 lux outdoors there will be an average of 500 lux inside. But the Daylight Factor should really be called the Skylight Factor because it ignores the sun. It takes no account of the orientation of a building or the local climate. The result is that windows often let in too much sunlight. To get an average of 5 per cent of the illuminance outdoors over a room requires a lot of glazing.

Designers sometimes do a separate set of calculations and work out how to control the sun in such circumstances. If not, the occupants may have to fight a constant battle to keep sunlight at bay, which often means drawing blinds or curtains. At the other extreme designers try and make sure that bright light or, rather, sunlight is intercepted at the perimeter of a building before it gets inside. Its intensity is lowered by shading or redirection so glare and solar heat gains are excluded. But if sunlight is kept out in this way the chances of someone inside being exposed to anything above about 2,000 lux are remote. What this approach overlooks is that one person's glare is another's phototherapy.

Direct sunlight is being designed out of modern buildings to prevent overheating and glare at the very time that scientists are showing that bright light is essential to our health. One reason this idea has taken so long to resurface, or to be rediscovered, is that before the 1970's very few studies had been done on it. There was little hard evidence that light at levels typically found outdoors had any influence on human physiology or behaviour. Most of the research, until this time, had been done using light levels required for vision, the ones that are typical of indoor lighting. Then, Dr. Alfred Lewy and co-workers at the National Institutes of Health in the USA published an article in *Science.* They reported that they could suppress the secretion of melatonin (the 'hormone of sleep' as it is sometimes called) by exposing subjects to bright artificial light. In the years that followed scientists found that people with seasonal cycles of depression respond favourably to light similar to outdoor levels, i.e. much higher than ordinary indoor intensity. In 1984, Dr. Norman Rosenthal, then of the National Institute of Mental Health, published an article in *Archives of General Psychiatry* about the seasonal pattern of depression that he called Seasonal Affective Disorder and described the relief of SAD with bright light. The symptoms of SAD take hold during the winter months and disappear in the summer, as the days get longer. They include lethargy, drowsiness, low levels of interest and concentration, and a craving for carbohydrates. Most people living at high latitudes experience some seasonal changes in their mood or behaviour, but SAD sufferers are seriously debilitated in the winter.

Following these discoveries doctors began to expose SAD patients to bright artificial light. They illuminated patients for 30 to 60 minutes in the morning with up to 10,000 lux from a white fluorescent light source. Responses varied from person-to-person but treatment early in the morning was often more effective at alleviating the symptoms than later in the day.

The Master Clock

There was, and still is, a great deal of scepticism about the effectiveness of bright light therapy for depression. One explanation for this is that clinical trials have not always been carried out as rigorously as they might have been. Another is there is no consensus as to how light therapy works. The biological mechanisms that underlie it are not clear, but they are becoming clearer. Each of us has a master clock, located at the centre of our brain. It resides in what are known as the suprachiasmatic nuclei (SCN) of the hypothalamus. This clock is entrained by cycles of light and dark and its job is to let the rest of the body know what time of day and what season it is. In very simple terms, when light reaches the retina at the back of the eye it is converted into electrical signals which travel along the optic nerve to the visual cortex at the rear of the brain. However, some of the nerve fibres branch off from the optic nerve soon after leaving the eye and these send signals to other parts of the brain, including the SCN. When the SCN is stimulated it passes a message to the hypothalamus' pineal gland to inhibit the secretion of melatonin which, in turn, tells us that we are biologically awake. Hormones such as melatonin are 'chemical messengers' that are made and secreted by specific glands and cells within the body. They pass via the bloodstream to target organs where they bind to receptor cells and deliver their 'message.' This elicits a biological response.

Our bodies have circadian clocks (*circa*, about; *diem*, a day) everywhere, not just in the brain but in the liver, in the lungs, in the stomach, in the skeletal muscles, and so on. Melatonin helps to entrain, or adapt, these internal clocks to the external environment. It is believed to be the primary hormone responsible for signalling biological processes, including our immune system. Melatonin is also a powerful antioxidant that helps the body to repair itself and fight off disease. Suppression of it during the day keeps us alert and encourages regular production of the same hormone during the hours of darkness, which is when we need it. If this cycle is disrupted and we secrete melatonin inappropriately, it affects our moods, sleep patterns and over time our general health. However, in order to make melatonin we first need to make its 'parent', the neurotransmitter serotonin. A neurotransmitter is a molecule in the brain that helps nerve cells to work together. Without enough serotonin to get brain cells to cooperate, and to make melatonin, a range of bodily functions can be disturbed, including mood.

Although it has been known since the 1980s that bright light affects melatonin secretion, the situation regarding serotonin – its precursor – was not so easy to work out. Autopsies showed that serotonin levels in peoples' brains are lowest in winter when SAD is at its worst. The antidepressant drugs commonly used to treat SAD, called SSRIs (selective serotonin re-uptake inhibitors) work by conserving the limited amount of serotonin there is in the brain. Yet concentrations of it appeared normal in SAD patients. This was because the standard technique for measuring serotonin involved taking samples from cerebrospinal fluid around the brain and spinal cord. This is an imprecise indicator of the brain's serotonergic activity. In 2002, in an article in *The Lancet*, researchers from the Baker Heart Research Institute in Australia reported that they had measured serotonin concentrations in blood vessels leading directly from the brain itself; giving a much more accurate assay. They found the rate of production of serotonin related directly to the amount of bright sunlight each day. It was higher on bright days than on overcast or cloudy ones. So, as of 2002, we know the turnover of serotonin in the brain significantly increases with sunlight both daily and seasonally. Levels of serotonin in the brain can be six times higher in the summer than in the winter. Sunlight helps us to manufacture serotonin each day and this, in turn, provides us with melatonin. Also, sunlight switches off the catalyst in the brain that converts serotonin to melatonin. So the sun turns serotonin on and melatonin off.

Research also suggests the spectral sensitivity of the entire circadian system is finely tuned to daylight. For about 150 years scientists thought the eye's visual photoreceptor cells – the rods and cones – did all of our light sensing. But in 2002 Dr. David Berson and co-researchers at Brown University found previously unknown light-sensing cells in the eye. These cells work in concert with the image-forming visual ones. But unlike them, they detect and respond to the general level of environmental lighting, rather than peaks and troughs, and they react slowly to luminance changes. In doing so, they provide the circadian system with a stable reading of average light levels, rather than the immediate response needed for vision. Also, they are sensitive to different wavelengths of light from rods and cones. Maximum sensitivity for our visual system lies in the yellow-green wavelength region, while the maximum biological sensitivity for these photoreceptor cells lies in the blue region of the spectrum. Much remains to be uncovered about them, and whatever their precise role they are especially sensitive to the wavelengths of light that are plentiful when there is a blue sky overhead. However, while blue light, or skylight may be particularly effective at suppressing the secretion of melatonin, skylight is not enough to keep us healthy. We also need to see sunlight to make its precursor serotonin, a lack of which is a factor in depression, anxiety, pain perception, and aggressive behaviour.

Serotonin also modulates blood pressure, metabolism and appetite. In 2006, researchers at the University of Pittsburgh discovered a connection between low serotonin levels and hardening of the arteries. They presented these results at a conference of the American Psychosomatic Society, which suggest that low serotonin levels in the brain may influence people to smoke or become physically inactive. Such lifestyle choices predispose them to arteriosclerosis. Or, poor lifestyle choices may lower serotonin levels in the brain, which then affects the neurotransmitter's role in modulating blood pressure, metabolism, and appetite. Either way, for the first time a link has been established between a lack of serotonin and heart disease. Research may be in its early stages, but one thing we can safely infer from all of the above is that lighting for vision is markedly different from biological lighting. Another inference is that we are better adapted to lighting conditions outdoors than those within. Unfortunately, most of us in the industrialized world spend too much time indoors to recognise this.

Sunlight Indoors

The human body's circadian system is like an antique clock. Very valuable. A thing of beauty even, but not as accurate as it could be. Its mechanism runs fast. So much so, every morning the minute hand has to be adjusted to keep the clock to good time. Otherwise, if kept under constant conditions, especially constant darkness, the master clock reverts to a rhythm that is more than 24 hours long. Without the proper time-cues needed to reset our internal clock it 'free-runs' and hormones start getting released at the wrong time and organs get the wrong message. Of course, rather than manual adjustments, we mostly rely on light to resynchronize or entrain ourselves with the light and dark cycles of the solar day. Sunlight is much brighter than skylight and so one might reasonably assume the impact of the sun on our circadian system is far greater than skylight. However, some scientists argue that it is the timing of the exposure, rather than the intensity of light, which is of critical importance. Light therapy during the early morning seems more effective than later in the day for many people. And it is also the case that domestic levels of light can influence the human circadian system. So too do regular mealtimes and other events during the day that are not related to light exposure. But, as we have already seen, it is sunlight, rather than skylight that relieves pain in hospital patients who have undergone surgery, and it is sunlight that stimulates liver function in babies.

Sunlight has also been shown to be of benefit to people in nursing homes who experience difficulty in sleeping at night. Normally the solution to disrupted sleep in the elderly is to give them medication in the form of sleeping pills, but an alternative approach is to let them see some sun. Artificial bright light therapy improves sleep patterns in the institutionalised elderly. But a study published in 2006 showed that nursing home residents who had about 30 to 60 minutes of direct sunlight each day experienced a significant improvement in sleep quality. They had less difficulty getting to sleep, woke less often during the night and enjoyed greater satisfaction with the sleep they got. When one considers that about 20 per cent of the population are affected by sleep disorders of one sort or another, this is a significant finding. Too little or too much sleep can have a negative impact on quality of life, safety, and productivity.

Research also shows that severely depressed hospital patients in sunlit rooms spend less time in hospital compared with patients in dull rooms. In 1996, Drs. Kathleen Beauchemin and Peter Hays were conducting a trial of light therapy at a psychiatric unit in Edmonton, Canada. They noticed that sunlight in some of the rooms was so bright as to overpower the effects of the light boxes they were using. On further inspection, they found that the psychiatric unit where the trial was taking place was sunny on one side and sunless and dull on the other. Reasoning the patients in the sunny rooms were inadvertently getting phototherapy, they looked through their medical records and at their lengths of stay. They found that severely depressed patients in sunny rooms were there for an average of 2.6 fewer days, or 15 per cent less time than those assigned to a dull room looking onto spaces in shadow.

Depression can be a life-threatening condition and this is due, in part, to the fact that individuals who develop it are at increased risk of heart disease. Also, people with heart disease are more likely to suffer from depression than healthy individuals. To further compound the problem, depression after a heart attack increases the risk of death. So, having discovered that sunny rooms helped clinically depressed patients to recover faster than dull ones, Drs. Beauchemin and Hayes then found that heart attack patients also benefit from being in sunlit wards. In 1998 they published a study in the *Journal of the Royal Society of Medicine* in which they examined the records of over six hundred patients admitted to a cardiac intensive care unit after a first heart attack. The study showed that deaths were more frequent among patients who were put in sunless north-facing rooms than among patients in sunlit rooms. In all, over a four year period, 39 died on the dark side and 21 on the bright side. They also discovered that sunlight affected women's recovery much more than men. The orientation of the men's rooms did not greatly influence the time they stayed in the cardiac unit before being discharged. But the amount of time women stayed there was. On average, women spent only 2.3 days in sunny rooms compared with 3.3 days in sunless rooms.

Women who develop heart disease generally do less well than men and this may be because they become depressed more commonly than men do. Also, seasonal affective disorder is chiefly a disorder of women. As of 2005, we know that bright light is as effective for seasonal and non-seasonal depression as medication. Sunlight may improve women's recovery from a heart attack simply by lifting them from a morbidly depressed mood. There is some support for this theory. In a study reported in the *Archives of General Psychiatry* in 2005, depressed patients who experienced a heart attack reduced their risk of a further attack or death if they took antidepressants, especially SSRIs. This was an accidental finding. The real aim of the research was to see if psychotherapy could help heart attack patients who suffer from depression, rather than whether antidepressant medication improves their chances of survival. Nevertheless, the results suggested that while psychotherapy had little effect, antidepressant drugs reduced the risk of death or a second heart attack by 43 per cent.

Sunlight may prevent heart attacks in a similar manner to antidepressants by alleviating depressive symptoms. Or there may be a combination of factors at work, as shown by the sun's impact on other conditions such as pain, jaundice and disturbed sleep patterns. Regardless of the exact mechanisms involved the fact that being in a sunlit ward may have health benefits is a significant finding which has profound implications; not least of which is the patients' survival from life-threatening conditions. On a more mercenary level there are the economics of healthcare to consider: faster recovery times mean lower costs. Findings such as these also bear out what Florence Nightingale believed about the influence of sunlight in patient recovery. In marked contrast to some of the leading doctors of her day, she believed that a view of the sky and especially sunlight was of the utmost importance to the sick. While subdued lighting was necessary for acute cases, a dark north room was inadmissible even for these. Miss Nightingale held that for nearly all hospital patients:

> ... the best rule is, if possible, give them direct sunlight from the moment he rises till the moment he sets.

Sunlight Outdoors

Unfortunately, today's design community is largely unaware of the benefits of sunlit spaces and so little regard is given to the health effects of sunlight either indoors, or outdoors. Where solar design is still practised, it is to save energy rather than prevent illnesses. At northerly latitudes the sun's rays are let into buildings to heat them up rather than keep the occupants well; and the underlying principles of doing so differ from those of designing to prevent disease. There is one feature in particular which distinguishes dwellings that exploit the therapeutic properties of sunlight from those simply arranged to capture the sun's rays to save energy. It is this: the exteriors of the former are arranged for the sun while the latter are not. Designing for health means, amongst other things, designing for sunbathing.

Window glass filters out the ultraviolet rays that synthesize vitamin D in our skin. So unless we are outside when the sun is above the horizon we will not generate any vitamin D. Years ago, hospitals had sun-terraces and balconies, and homes had sunrooms and verandas. Now they do not, and skin-cancer campaigns have bred such a fear of ultraviolet radiation that many see the sun simply as something that ages them, causes cancer and must be avoided. It is now ingrained in us to think twice before going out in sunlight. Yet, for most of human history, mankind has revered the sun as a source of light, life and health, and for good reason. The less sunlight we get, the less vitamin D we make in our bodies. This, in turn, means that we cannot absorb the calcium and the other ingredients in our diets we need to keep our bones in good order and ensure our nerves and muscles work effectively. Lack of sunlight has long been associated with weak bones, weak muscles and ill health. *'Where the sun does not go the doctor does'*, as an old Italian saying has it.

Until recently most doctors thought vitamin D was narrow acting and that its only value was in skeletal development and bone mineralization. More and more evidence is coming to light, which shows that vitamin D plays a central role in maintaining a healthy immune system. Research suggests that low levels of vitamin D may be linked to many chronic and potentially fatal diseases that are not related to bone health. It seems that every organ and every cell in the human body needs vitamin D to work properly. The primary source of it for most of us is the sun. This means our immune systems may be seriously compromised if we stay indoors when the sun is out. And just at the time that scientists are discovering how pivotal vitamin D is to our health, others are beginning to recognise how common vitamin D deficiency is. Unfortunately, the undue focus on the harmful effects of the sun's ultraviolet rays in recent years has rather overshadowed the benefits they can bring and the dangers of not getting enough of them.

Sunlight and Vitamin D

Vitamin D is not a vitamin at all. It is a prohormone. Vitamins are substances that cannot normally be synthesised in the body and have to be provided in the diet. But we can make all the vitamin D we need by going out in sunshine, if it's strong enough. Our skin has a high concentration of cholesterol in it that is converted by enzymes into a sterol, called 7-dehydrocholesterol. When the sun's photons hit the skin they trigger the photochemical conversion of 7-dehydrocholesterol into vitamin D3. This travels to the liver where it is transformed into 25-hydroxyvitamin D3 , the form of vitamin D that circulates in the blood. Some of this then passes to the kidneys which converts it into 1,25-hydroxyvitamin D3, the biologically active form of vitamin D that provides all the health benefits we hear about. This is also called calcitriol and sometimes soltriol, which means 'hormone of sunlight'. Soltriol travels from the kidneys to the intestines, where it promotes calcium absorption and helps maintain healthy blood calcium levels. Until recently the kidneys were thought to be the only organs that could activate 25-hydroxyvitamin D3 into soltriol. Then research showed that humans have the ability to make activated vitamin D throughout the body. Cells in the breast, colon, prostate, brain, skin and elsewhere make their own 1,25-hydroxyvitamin D3, or soltriol. Unlike the activated vitamin D made in the kidneys, which promotes bone health, vitamin D activated in other organs and tissues ensures cells grow properly. It controls the way they develop. When there isn't enough 25-hydroxyvitamin D3 to convert into soltriol it becomes easier for cancer cells to reproduce and spread. Also, soltriol influences immune-cell activity, which explains why vitamin D plays an important part in preventing infectious diseases such as tuberculosis and immune-related disorders. These include diabetes, multiple sclerosis, and rheumatoid arthritis. Unfortunately, no one knows how much vitamin D the human body needs to stay healthy – a subject we will return to later.

At this point it might be worth looking at what the sun's much-maligned rays do besides triggering the synthesis of vitamin D in the skin, and serotonin in the brain. Sunlight stimulates the production of dopamine and endorphins, two more of our 'feel-good' hormones. Sunlight boosts the production of cortisone, a hormone that controls a range of functions including our anti-inflammatory immune response. And sunlight increases testosterone levels in men, about which perhaps the less said the better. Ultraviolet radiation from the sun will lower blood pressure, reduce cholesterol levels, reduce blood sugar levels, increase cardiac output, increase the oxygen content of the blood and can strengthen the immune system. This explains why sunlight has been used as a medicine for thousands of years and why in the 1920s and 30s public health recommendations on sunbathing were diametrically opposed to those being made at present. In those days doctors routinely recommended sunbathing for a wide variety of diseases. Ironically it is only now, when sunlight therapy has all but disappeared, that many of the same diseases are being shown to be associated with vitamin D deficiency. There is compelling evidence that sunlight exposure prevents many more deaths than it causes. Much of this has been ignored because it is unfashionable and largely based on epidemiologic studies (surveys of population groups) rather than scientifically conducted randomized, double blind studies. There have been precious few clinical trials of vitamin D over the last 50 years, probably because its action was thought to be so limited. Nevertheless laboratory research is now confirming just how important maintaining adequate levels of vitamin D is.

Healthy Darkness

It is also becoming clear that while we need bright light during the day to keep ourselves in step with the sun's 24-hour cycle, we also need darkness at night. This is because exposure to light at night disrupts the secretion of melatonin, a hormone which, in a similar manner to vitamin

D, has been shown to have anticancer properties. Several studies point to an association between light exposure at night and an increased risk of breast and colorectal cancer. This increased risk may be related to the suppression of nocturnal melatonin secretion. A possible explanation is that one of melatonin's many functions is to trigger a decrease in the body's oestrogen levels at night. Some researchers have speculated that chronically decreasing nocturnal melatonin production might increase an individual's risk of developing oestrogen-related malignancies, such as breast cancer. Evidence now exists that indirectly links exposures to light at night to human breast and colorectal cancers in shift workers. So while it is important for us to see some bright light during the day, it may be equally important to remain in total darkness at night.

The human circadian and neuroendocrine system is acutely sensitive to the blue wavelengths in white light at this time. This means that exposure to even the most minute amounts of white light at night can negatively affect sleep quality, and lower the effectiveness of the immune system. Unfortunately, much of the modern urban environment is lit throughout the nighttime which puts darkness at something of a premium. Lighting up our towns and cities at night may have had some very adverse and unforeseen consequences for health. Until recently, medical science overlooked the suppression of melatonin by light at night as a contributer to the overall incidence of cancer and other diseases. It could be significant. More people now work at night than ever before and may be compromising their health by doing so. The idea that light at night is 'light pollution' is gaining ground and becoming a public health issue, although it is unlikely that the street lamps and neon signs will go off just yet. Scientists are still working out how and when to limit light at night and are trying to identify lighting practices that will best safeguard human health.

With the precautionary principle in mind, it might be prudent to sleep in total darkness if possible. There is some evidence that red, orange or amber wavelengths may be less disruptive to normal sleep patterns than blue wavelengths. Red lighting is used to preserve night vision which may, or may not, be significant in this context. Until we know more, anyone who has to put lights on at night to go to the bathroom or elsewhere might be wise to use a red lamp. This could minimize the disruption of their circadian systems and maintain their melatonin secretion. One other thing to consider is that although we need to be in bright light during the day, in the evening we need a more subdued lighting regime to prepare our circadian system for its nocturnal duties.

Light and the Eye

And now a word of caution: while bright light can be good for us at certain times during the day, prolonged gazing at very bright sources, especially those emitting shorter wavelength blue light, can cause damage to the retina at the back of the eye. This results in temporary or permanent loss of visual acuity. Watching the sun as it rises and sets is safe enough for most of us, but staring at it gets dangerous within an hour of its rising and remains so until roughly an hour before it sets. Too much sunlight damages the retina and can cause blindness. Fortunately such an event would normally be prevented by our natural aversion response, which is to close our eyes or look away from a light source if it is too strong. Unfortunately for some individuals the temptation to look at a solar eclipse with the naked eye can prove too much. Permanent damage, including blindness, is often the result. Other symptoms of acute exposure to the sun's rays include photoconjunctivitis and photokeratitis, or inflammation of conjuctiva and cornea of the eye respectively. However, the extent to which chronic sun exposure is a significant risk factor for cataracts is unclear, as is also the case both for macular degeneration and melanoma of the eye, two other conditions often attributed to the sun.

In common with sunlight, bright light emitted from lamps and some overhead fixtures can be harmful if looked at for too long. In the 1950s and 1960s, when some of the more influential studies on electric lighting and visual comfort were carried out, much of the emphasis was on the elimination of glare. Designers were encouraged to specify luminaires that limited the intensity of light or diffused it. Such an approach largely eliminated the problem but resulted in rooms having a gloomy underlit appearance. People who work in this sort of environment, which continues to be typical of offices and many other building types, can usually see well enough. They can carry out their tasks in safety and with reasonable visual comfort. But what light they do get usually comes from above. The light boxes used for SAD and other medical conditions provide the viewer with a diffuse source rather than a direct beam. They simulate skylight rather than sunlight. Patients position themselves so that the light is in their peripheral vision and can glance into it. The dosage they get is many times higher than that of normal indoor lighting and, unlike most indoor lighting, it is emitted at eye-level. This is significant because where the entrainment of the circadian system is concerned it is the amount of light that reaches the photoreceptors in the retina at the back of the eye that matters and not the ambient lighting level. Sitting next to a light box which delivers 2,500 lux to the eye will present the circadian system with far more stimulus than 2,500 lux from an overhead light fitting. What this means as far as interior lighting is concerned is that the best way to entrain our biological rhythms during the day appears to be to provide areas of higher illuminance at eye level, or where it will be frequently viewed, rather than providing a general increase in illuminance throughout interiors. A more traditional approach to the problem would be to simply let in more sunshine at the right time.

Chapter 3
Depressed? You soon will be

Depression is a debilitating, persistent, and sometimes deadly disease, and it is becoming more common. Scientists don't know why this steady increase is happening. But if bright light can cure major depression then – as Aretaeus observed all those years ago – gloom and lack of sunlight may play an important, if largely unrecognised, part in it. The marked increase in depression during the second half of the 20th century coincides with a mass migration indoors to low light levels and, more recently, with public health campaigns promoting sun-avoidance. Whether our subterranean lifestyles are in any way to blame is uncertain. Some commentators say there has been no real increase in depression over the last 50 years. They argue the statistics simply reflect a greater willingness on the public's part to admit to suffering from the condition and to seek help for it. Modern society attaches less stigma to this form of mental illness than was once the case. Others argue there is more depression these days simply because doctors diagnose it far more readily than they used to. They have SSRIs and other drugs at their disposal that alleviate the symptoms with fewer damaging side effects than previous generations of antidepressants. Whatever the truth behind the statistics, the fact remains that depression is the cause of more hospital admissions than any other psychiatric disorder.

So how common is it? Some 340 million people worldwide suffer from depression, including 18 million in the United States alone. In 2003, the authors of a paper published in the *British Journal of Psychiatry* estimated that 6 per cent of the British population meet the criteria for major depression at any time. About 20 per cent of those with a major depressive illness will have symptoms that persist beyond 2 years. Whether increasing or not, this disabling and potentially life-threatening condition can be devastating for sufferers and their families. The disorder can be long-lasting and highly recurrent. A third of these patients experience a relapse within three months of recovery and, if they do not continue treatment, 50 per cent experience a further episode within 2 years. Depression is especially dangerous for men. Although they are less likely to suffer from it than women, men do not fare as well – perhaps because they are less inclined to ask for help. According to a review published in the *Journal of Clinical Psychiatry* in 2001, between 40 to 80 per cent of people suffering with depression do not seek treatment for their illness. Of those who do, less than 10 per cent are likely to receive adequate care.

Depression comes in several forms: as major, or clinical, depression; as manic depression, otherwise known as bipolar disorder; as dysthymia, or dysthymic disorder, which is a less severe, but more chronic form of clinical depression; and as seasonal affective disorder. Depressive symptoms that fall short of a diagnosis of a depressive disorder are also common: mild to moderate depression is more prevalent in the community than severe depression. As far as the seasonal form of the condition is concerned, somewhere between four and ten per cent of people in countries at northerly latitudes suffer from it. Taken together, SAD and the milder form of it, the so-called 'winter blues', may affect as much as 20 per cent of populations depending on how far from the equator they live.

Both seasonal and non-seasonal depression respond to bright light therapy. But the medical profession continues to regard the treatment of depression as a chemical problem, and turns to medication when confronted by it. Although the most widely prescribed antidepressants, SSRIs, are more benign than their predecessors, they can still produce some very unpleasant and dangerous side-effects. A significant minority of people who take them experience an increase in suicidal thoughts, while severe withdrawal symptoms are common. Bright light therapy offers a safe, inexpensive alternative to drugs, although this is still not a popular approach to treatment. Indeed, even SAD is not recognised as a medical condition in some quarters. A contributor to the *British Journal of Psychiatry* in 2003 observed that:

> ... *many psychiatrists seem to doubt its existence. Disbelievers aver that apparent winter depression is a temporal coincidence among some people with recurrent affective disorder. More ardent opponents of the diagnosis accuse psychiatrists of helping to promulgate another condition, popularised by the media, which merely adds a further weapon to the hypochondriac's armamentarium.*

This is not altogether surprising given that modern medical training fails to acquaint psychiatrists, or doctors in general, with the history of their art. They are unused to thinking about cyclical influences on health. Like the rest of us, they are shielded from major changes in their environment and from the sun for much of the time. If they were more familiar with medical history, and the sun's influence on human affairs, they might be a little more open to the idea that there are seasonal patterns to depression and other diseases.

The scepticism which surrounds the use of bright light to treat depression is, to a degree, more understandable. Many of the studies published on the efficacy of light therapy have been methodologically flawed in one way or another, raising doubts whether bright light is truly effective for SAD or for non-seasonal depression. One reason for these shortcomings is that multinational companies do not fund trials that do not involve drugs, such as those for light therapy. So sample sizes tend to be small, often fewer than 20 patients, and the duration of treatment much shorter than would be the case with well-resourced clinical trials.

Fortunately, for those seeking scientific proof of the positive effects of bright light on mood disorders, a study commissioned by the American Psychiatric Association, published in the *American Journal of Psychiatry* in April 2005, concluded that light therapy is as effective as medication in treating depression. A research team assessed the evidence base for the efficacy of light therapy in treating mood disorders. They conducted a statistical analysis of 20 studies published in scientific and medical journals over a 20 year period that were deemed rigorous enough to be included in their review. A further 153 were either too unsound or poorly designed to produce scientifically reliable results and so were rejected. The 20 well-designed studies showed bright light therapy to be an effective treatment not only for SAD but also for major depression.

There is also good evidence that a technique called 'dawn simulation' is effective for SAD sufferers. Instead of waking to the sound of an alarm clock, they can programme a device to create an artificial dawn that begins 60 to 90 minutes before waking. This produces a gradual increase in light levels to a maximum of about 500 lux. So it seems the lighting conditions an hour or so before sunrise can be therapeutic. But why dawn simulation achieves similar results to bright light therapy is not known.

Meanwhile, what of the conventional approach to depression? There has been much concern about adverse reactions to the medications used to treat it. For many years, SSRI antidepressants were commonly used in child and adolescent psychiatry until questions were raised about their efficacy and safety. In 2005, the authors of a paper in the Dutch medical journal *Nederlands Tijdschrift voor Geneeskunde* commented on an increase in suicidal behaviour among young people taking SSRIs. They argued that these drugs should not be prescribed for depression in children and adolescents; and that an initially positive attitude towards administering SSRIs within the medical community arose because of both the lack of a critical attitude by authors and editors of scientific journals, as well as a lack of candidness by the pharmaceutical industry. Others disagree, and maintain that SSRIs have reduced suicide levels in this age group. Drug therapy is a more profitable way of dealing with depression than light therapy and is likely to remain the treatment of choice for adults until phototherapy gains wider acceptance.

Sunlight, Suicide and Serotonin

About 15 per cent of people with major depression commit suicide. The idea that anyone taking an antidepressant could feel more inclined to take their lives is disconcerting. Light therapy has few such side effects and works more quickly than drugs. Oral antidepressants can take four to six weeks to start working. In most cases, light therapy begins to work within the first four to seven days. Also, light therapy is well tolerated. While there can be adverse effects such as eye strain and headache, these seldom lead to the cessation of the treatment.

Yet, paradoxically, there is a darker side to the sun where depression is concerned. Although SAD sufferers gain relief from their symptoms in the summer months, sunlight at this time of year is associated with suicide; although not in quite the same way as SSRIs. Suicidal behaviour follows a consistent seasonal pattern worldwide, with more deaths in the early summer than at any other time of year. In Britain, more people take their lives in May than in any other month. Research suggests that suicides peak in the summer because people with depression experience a partial remission at this time of year. Seemingly, bright sunlight gives them just enough serotonin and sufficient energy to carry out a suicide plan. With all that is known about sunlight lifting negative mood states this seems a little perverse. However, an explanation for this curious phenomenon appeared in the *Journal of Affective Disorders* in 2005. It seems that when sunshine acts as a natural antidepressant it does so in two stages: first it improves motivation; then only later does it improve mood. The time lag from the initial burst of energy sunlight gives to the improved state of mind that follows may be as much as nine days. This is a dangerously long time in which to feel depressed and yet motivated enough to do something about it. Whether the hypothesis proves to be correct or not, for susceptible individuals the summer sun brings with it a potential short-term increased risk of suicide, which deserves to be more widely recognised. If nothing else, the seasonal increase in suicide underscores the ancient belief in the cyclical nature of illnesses.

While suicide poses the most immediate threat to someone with severe depression, the dangers do not end there. Depression can have a damaging effect on the body, compromising the integrity of the immune system and increasing susceptibility to acute diseases, such as colds, influenza, or other types of infection. And it can cause significant functional disability, making it difficult to perform the normal tasks of daily life and to engage in social activities. While heart disease is the chronic disorder most closely associated with depression, there are others such as multiple sclerosis, hypertension, diabetes, rheumatoid arthritis, cancer and low bone mineral density. As with heart disease these occur more frequently where there is less sunlight. All of the conditions in this list have been linked to a deficiency of the hormone of the sun, vitamin D. We know that sunlight lifts the spirits, even if it takes a few days to do so, but what about vitamin D and depression? In tests, people with low levels of it score highly for depressive symptoms; and there is evidence that vitamin D improves mood and well-being.

Scientists have found there are receptors for 1,25-dihydroxyvitamin D_3 in the brain, and clinical and experimental data indicate that vitamin D may affect cerebral function, in particular, signalling between nerve cells. One intriguing finding is the difference that consumption of fish oils around the world has on depression. Countries with a low level of fish consumption are reported to have a higher prevalence of major depression. A number of studies have reported a reduced level of omega-3 fatty acids in the plasma or red blood cells of depressed patients. However, so far there are no studies in the literature showing vitamin D will lift someone out of a major depression in the way that bright light can.

Most of our vitamin D comes from the sun; and the sun is also responsible for increasing serotonin levels in the brain. Both serotonin and vitamin D improve our sense of well-being and vitality, but the relationship between them is unclear. In 1998, scientists at the University of Helsinki put forward the idea that the amount of serotonin available to us in the winter is determined by our exposure to sunlight during the previous summer. The idea behind this was that vitamin D stored in the body helps to maintain higher levels of serotonin during the winter months, and that soaking up the sun in the summer may prevent or reduce depression during the winter. This would help to explain why suicides are more common in the early summer when reserves of vitamin D and, thus, serotonin may still be low following the winter hiatus. Things are never as straightforward as they appear, however. Although serotonin levels have something to do with regulating mood, they are not the cause of depression. People with low levels of serotonin do not necessarily become depressed. So the closer one looks at sunlight, serotonin and vitamin D the more complicated it all becomes.

One of the symptoms that distinguish SAD from other forms of depression is a craving for carbohydrates, especially sweets, and a tendency to put on weight following their consumption. This craving may be a signal from the body that its serotonin levels are depleted or out of balance and that, without sunlight, the solution is a change of diet. To deal with a large intake of carbohydrate, the body secretes insulin to reduce the raised blood sugar levels that ensue. In doing so, it also helps an amino acid in the diet called tryptophan to reach the brain, where it is converted into serotonin. The boost in serotonin levels that follows carbohydrate consumption gives a temporary feeling of comfort and well-being. But serotonin gained this way, courtesy of sweets and potatoes, comes at the price of an increase in waistline. This tendency to use carbohydrates as though they were drugs and to self-medicate is also characteristic of women with premenstrual syndrome, and of people trying to give up smoking.

Foods such as turkey, milk, whole grains, bananas and eggs are good sources of tryptophan, and hence serotonin and then melatonin. There is another substance called 5-hydroxytryptophan (5-HTP) which is a more immediate precursor to serotonin than tryptophan. This is available over the counter as a dietary supplement and is used as a natural antidepressant. It is sometimes used by SAD sufferers who do not respond to light therapy. An alternative to the dietary approach to lifting depression is to take regular physical exercise, which can be as effective as prescription drugs for mild to moderate cases. There are several explanations for this, the most obvious of which is that physical activity alters brain chemistry and so produces a mood-elevating effect. Exercise activates hormones and neurotransmitters in the body, one of which is serotonin. There is even evidence that regular exercise combats depression by influencing the body's circadian clock in some way. Of course, there are psychological benefits too, such as an increased sense of self-worth, and opportunities to meet new people and overcome the social withdrawal that is a common symptom of the disorder. Taken together, these and other benefits explain why people who have depression and take exercise for it have significantly lower relapse rates than people taking medication, and that continued exercise is associated with lower rates of depression.

Exercise and Light

Significantly, when regular exercise and bright light are combined the psychological benefits increase. Research published in the *Journal of Affective Disorders* in 2002 shows that exercise is a much more effective antidepressant when taken with exposure to light at levels above about 2,500 lux. This is roughly the amount of light outdoors on an overcast winter's day. Outdoor light in winter on its own is intense enough at higher latitudes to alleviate the symptoms of SAD, providing sufferers stay outside for an hour or more in the morning. But when combined with exercise, bright-light exposure can be limited to 30 minutes just three times a week and still has a positive effect on mood and health-related quality of life. A regime of this kind is effective for people with subthreshold depression, or subsyndromal seasonal symptoms in the wintertime; which is about 20 per cent of the adult population in temperate regions.

Some of the more forward-thinking architects of the last century provided their clients with terraces and open-air balconies where they could exercise in natural light. Although they were not aware that this had a synergistic effect on mood and serotonin levels, they were alert to the health benefits. Unfortunately, today few people spend enough time outdoors to have any impact on their physical or mental well-being. This is evident from the amount of outdoor light the middle-aged residents of San Diego, California get each day. A study published in *Biological Psychiatry* in 1994, showed that San Diegans were only in daylight at levels greater than 1000 lux for about 4 per cent of the time, or 58 minutes a day on average. If people living in one of the sunnier regions of the United States limit their time in bright light to this extent then those of us living further north are likely to be equally light-deprived, perhaps even more so. Indeed, some of us spend so much time indoors that we have to invest in light boxes to compensate for lack of sunlight.

Depression places a large financial burden on society – especially in the workplace. Figures published in the *British Journal of Psychiatry* put the cost of depression in England in 2000 at more than £9 billion a year. Only £370 million of this total was due to direct treatment costs, such as medication and counselling. Of the rest, £8.1 billion was accounted for by the 109 million working days lost to the condition. These figures do not include the hidden impact of depression on reduced productivity at work: an impact that is not measured by absenteeism rates. In the United States the economic burden was $83.1 billion in 2000, of which $26.1 billion were direct medical costs, $51.5 billion were workplace costs, and $5.4 billion were suicide-related. How much of this is attributable to lack of exercise and under-exposure to the sun is anyone's guess. But offices, factories, hospitals or any other type of building that do not allow access to bright light are not going to help matters. Nor are housing developments that do not include parks and recreation areas where residents can exercise in daylight, rather than indoors under fluorescent tubes. As we shall see in Chapter 8, the pioneers of the Modern Movement were convinced there was a direct link between town planning, housing, sunlight and health. They designed to prevent disease. Today this no longer applies. In many countries, national policies on health and the built environment have become entirely divorced, and have different aims. As far as buildings are concerned, governments seem more interested in reducing their impact on the environment than on improving the well-being of the people inside them. Meanwhile, health policy is largely directed towards treating disease rather than preventing it. Within health care services, poor housing does not feature prominently, because the link between housing and disorders such as depression is not accepted, or is not seen as a healthcare responsibility. Building design, housing improvement and town planning are not regarded as health interventions in themselves. Imhotep might have had something to say about this.

Depression and Obesity

It is difficult to establish the impact of any individual measure on so complex a disorder as depression. But it seems reasonable to suggest that where spaces are sunlit, where outdoor recreational activities flourish, and where walking and cycling the norm rather than the exception, there might be a little less of it about. There is scientific evidence that the built environment has a direct impact on depression and other forms of mental illness. Poor-quality housing increases psychological distress, but the underlying causes are proving hard to pin down. By contrast, where physical diseases are concerned the evidence is compelling. Around two-thirds of the English population are now overweight or obese. According to a report of the House of Commons Health Committee in 2004, based on present trends, obesity will soon overtake smoking as the greatest cause of premature loss of life. It will bring levels of sickness in its wake that may make Britain's publicly funded health service unsustainable. The adverse effects of being overweight include diabetes, gall bladder disease, heart attack, stroke, colon cancer, high blood pressure and osteoarthritis, as well as an increase in early mortality. If the latest predictions are correct we are going to see a one-third increase in the loss of healthy life as a result of obesity over the next 20 years. The number of global deaths each year will rise from three million to five million. The economic burden of obesity is comparable to that of depression. Figures for the United States in 1995 show the indirect costs of obesity were $47.6 billion and the direct costs $51.2 billion. And matters have not improved: there are more obese Americans now than there were then. In 2000, the WHO estimated the total cost attributable to obesity and its negative health impacts represent 2 to 7 per cent of national health spending worldwide. The relative contributions of diet and activity to this global crisis remain unclear, but town planning has undoubtedly played its part. As the House of Commons Health Committee noted in their report:

> The increasing use of cars has led to a vicious circle of car dependency, as town planning has increasingly prioritised the needs of motorists above those of pedestrians and cyclists, meaning that in many places walking and cycling are at best unpleasant and at worst dangerous. At the same time, local neighbourhoods are increasingly perceived by parents as unsafe for children to play out in, implicitly discouraging active play and forcing children back in front of the television set. This phenomenon was repeatedly described by our witnesses.

That the modern built environment can determine a person's prospects for being overweight is beyond doubt. According to the findings of a study published in the *American Journal of Preventive Medicine* in 2004, the most significant design factor for obesity is the number of shops, offices, and other varied destinations within walking distance of home. Researchers tracked the travel behaviour of more than 10,500 people in Atlanta, Georgia, and assessed the layout of the streets near to where they lived, and their body weight. The results showed that where land use changed from neighbourhoods comprising only houses to ones that included shops or services, the likelihood of obesity fell by seven per cent. For individual residents, this meant their relative chance of being obese dropped by 35 per cent. The results of this study also showed that driving a motor vehicle can be a major risk factor and that every additional 30 minutes spent in one translates into a three per cent greater chance of being obese. People are less likely to drive and more likely to walk if they live in neighbourhoods with a mix of uses. To this end, planners need to get more people out of their motors and on to the streets by putting shops and other facilities within walking distance of their homes, and by making walking and cycling convenient and safe.

However, urban planning and building design alone will not solve our obesity problems. People in poorer neighbourhoods are especially susceptible to obesity because they often perceive the environment in which they live as hostile and threatening thanks to litter, graffiti, discarded injection equipment, a risk of muggings and assaults, and disturbances from youths. Such 'incivilities' are likely to deter them from walking or cycling around in the local area, or letting their children play outside. Research published in the *British Journal of Sports Medicine* in 2000, shows that people in poorer areas lack safe open green spaces where they can walk, jog, or take their children to play, which limits their opportunities for exercise. Simply planning parks, playgrounds and cycle paths and putting shops within walking distance of houses is not enough. Residents have to feel happy about using them – which brings us back to depression. Regular exercise relieves the symptoms of depression, while lack of exercise can bring it on, and one way it does so is via obesity. The obese are often unhappy about their weight and can become clinically depressed as a result. The relationship may be circular, each relating to the other. Low serotonin levels in depressed patients cause them to eat meals high in carbohydrates; and overweight individuals report eating more when anxious or depressed. And just to make a complex subject even more so, weight gain is linked to sun exposure, or a lack of it. Sunlight stimulates the production of a hormone in the brain and skin called alpha-melanocyte stimulating hormone (alphaMSH). Research suggests that this is a powerful appetite suppressant; and that it may be involved in obesity. In experiments, elevated levels of this hormone reduce body weight and body fat. Similarly, vitamin D will normalise food intake and blood sugar levels, and obesity is associated with vitamin D deficiency. Studies show that the human body accumulates fat as vitamin D levels fall. Also, excess fat in the body absorbs and retains vitamin D and prevents it from exerting its effects on energy metabolism, muscle strength and so on, making physical activity even more difficult than it already is for overweight people. Lack of sunlight may be a factor in the seemingly inexorable tide of obesity; and depression too. By now it may come as no surprise to learn that in the ancient world, doctors used sunlight therapy for corpulence as well as depression. Scientific evidence may emerge which shows they were right to do so. If planning neighbourhoods to encourage physical activity can prevent obesity, planning them for sunlight might improve matters even further.

Chapter 4
Vitamin D Deficiency
The Silent Epidemic

Climate Change is not a new phenomenon. Planet Earth has warmed up and cooled down on a number of occasions and no doubt will do so again. At the beginning of the 17th century the winters in England were particularly severe. It was so cold in London that the River Thames froze over. No one knows why the temperature fell so much but it may have been because the sun's output was unusually low at this time. A prolonged period of global cooling, the so-called Little Ice Age, lasted from about 1300 to 1850 and reached its coldest point at about the same time as an event known as the Maunder Minimum.

Under normal circumstances the sun shows signs of variability, such as its eleven-year sunspot cycle. But a 19th-century solar astronomer, E. W. Maunder (1851–1928) worked out from a detailed examination of the Royal Observatory's records that between the years 1645 and 1715 there had been almost no sunspot activity at all. Whether this unusual hiatus was accompanied by a net fall in the sun's energy is still a matter of some debate among astronomers. But medical literature published in England during the Maunder Minimum supports the theory that solar radiation was scarce at this time. Doctors began to notice that within a few months of birth babies were becoming weak and sickly, with stunted growth. They suffered bone pain or pain with movement and were susceptible to muscular spasms, fractures, anorexia, and weight loss. Their bones were soft causing deformities of the spine and limbs, such as bowed legs or knocked knees, or bowing of the long bones in the arms. These symptoms were seen so often that doctors began writing about them.

In 1650, Dr. Francis Glisson published a famous treatise on this mysterious condition in which he described its clinical and anatomic features in great detail. Like other physicians of the day, Dr. Glisson thought that it was a new disease and struggled to identify why it was affecting so many infants. But it was not new: in about AD 100 the first account of it that matches current clinical descriptions was written by Soranus of Ephesus. He described what was to become recognised as the classic disease of vitamin D deficiency, namely, rickets. Unfortunately, there is nothing in the surviving writings of Soranus to suggest that he used sunlight to treat rickets, or that he recognised the importance of sunlight exposure in preventing it. Dr. Glisson certainly did not, and there were to be no advances in the study of rickets in the 200 years that followed the publication of Glisson's treatise, during which time the disease became endemic. The Maunder Minimum passed, but the industrial age that followed it compounded the problem. Countless children died or were left permanently crippled by the condition and

mothers, who had developed the disease in childhood, and had pelvic deformities as a result, had to undergo caesarean sections, or died in childbirth. There are no precise figures for the mortality from rickets because it killed indirectly. So officially deaths were recorded as one of its many complications. These include pneumonia, whooping cough and other respiratory infections. In 1915, an examination of schoolchildren in the East End of London found that rickets affected 80 per cent of them, while studies in the USA and elsewhere in Europe showed similar results. Although some doctors used sunlight to treat it, there was

Fig. 6. Rickets
(Wellcome LIbrary, London)

still much uncertainty as to the cause of the disease. Unfortunately, no one within the mainstream of medicine considered sunlight deprivation to be a factor.

Over the years a number of theories were put forward in an attempt to explain why rickets was so common. One was that it was the result of an inadequate diet; another that it was an hereditary disease; a third was that it was caused by syphilis or an unidentified bacterial infection. Then there was the 'domestication' theory, which held that rickets was caused by a combination of bad hygiene and confinement indoors. Some doctors attributed it to a lack of fresh air and exercise. Others argued that rickets was the result of changes in 'internal secretions'. In 1918 the

Medical Research Committee of Great Britain reviewed these and other theories in a very detailed investigation. They reached the following conclusion:

> ...in spite of the most varied and extensive research we have
> practically no real knowledge of the nature or causation of
> this widespread malady or the factors which determine its
> onset.

Nevertheless, the disease was well known as a seasonal condition that appeared in the winter and early spring and then healed in the summer. Also, the relationship between rickets and sunlight exposure had been documented 100 years earlier. In 1815, the French doctor Cauvin had recommended sunlight exposure as a treatment for rickets. Then in 1822 the great Polish scientist and physician, Professor Jedrzej Sniadecki (1768–1838) wrote of the importance of the sun's rays in preventing and curing the 'English Disease' as it had become known on the Continent. In 1862 another French physician, Dr. Armand Trousseau, argued that rickets was a disease brought about by nutritional deficiency and a sunless climate. In 1890 Dr. Theobald Palm, a general practitioner in the north of England surveyed the geographical distribution of rickets around the world. He showed that despite a superior diet and better sanitary conditions, Britain's infants were at much greater risk from the disease than infants living in poorer countries. Earlier in his career Dr. Palm had practised medicine in Japan where rickets was almost unknown. In a masterly investigation, which was years ahead of its time he consulted medical missionaries in India, Japan, China, and other parts of the world and showed that countries immune to rickets enjoyed plentiful sunshine and clear skies. Britain, in contrast, suffered grey skies, frequent fogs and a lack of sunshine. The effects were intensified in towns that, thanks to the Industrial Revolution, were under:

> ... a perennial pall of smoke, and where the high houses cut
> off from streets a large proportion of the rays which struggle
> through the gloom.

It was in the narrow alleys where the children of the poor played that this exclusion was worst, and it was here that most victims of rickets could be found. Dr. Palm published a paper in the medical journal *The Practitioner* in which he concluded that the disease occurred because of deprivation of sunlight. He put forward several measures to eliminate the disease. They included the removal of rickety children from large towns to sanatoriums in sunlit places; and the systematic use of sun baths as a preventative and therapeutic measure in rickets and other diseases. Dr.

Palm argued for the education of the public to the appreciation of sunlight as a means of health:

> *Many persons seem to prefer darkness to light in their dwellings out of ignorance, thoughtlessness, or even an economic regard for carpets and curtains. Let people understand that sun-light in the dwelling not only reveals unsuspected dirt, but is nature's universal disinfectant, as well as a stimulant and tonic. Such knowledge will also stimulate efforts for the abatement of smoke and the multiplication of open spaces, especially as playgrounds for the children of the poor.*

Dr. Palm's paper aroused no interest whatever, and it was to be more than 30 years before his recommendations were adopted. During the intervening period others noticed that sunlight prevented the disease and a few tried to do something about it. The Swiss physician Dr. Auguste Rollier (1874–1954) published a book on sunlight therapy in 1916 in which he wrote that the sun cure was 'without doubt' the treatment of choice in rickets. But it was not until 1921 that scientists finally proved to everyone's satisfaction that rickets develops when children are deprived of sunlight, and that sunbathing cures it. Given an oversight of such enormity and such tragic results it is ironic that the elimination of rickets is regarded as one of the great medical triumphs of the 20th century. Doubly so, since this is usually attributed to the introduction of vitamin D supplements into the diet, rather than sun exposure. The promotion of sunbathing as a public health measure began during the 1920s along the lines that Dr. Palm had suggested in 1890. This raises a number of questions, but one in particular. Why did the medical establishment either overlook, or ignore, sunlight as the primary factor in the aetiology of this crippling bone disease for 300 years? Part of the answer is that from the Fall of Rome until the 1920s few doctors considered sun exposure to be therapeutic for rickets or anything else. Also rickets was a childhood disease and, as such, of no great concern to the profession. Children who were well enough went into factories, down mines or up chimneys. Those crippled by disease begged on the streets. Interest in child welfare did grow during the Industrial Revolution. But the general view seems to have been that if handicapped children survived into adulthood they would not be useful members of society and therefore little provision was made for them. And there were also centuries of prejudice to overcome.

Charles Dickens and the Sun

In mediaeval times the lame had been treated with suspicion, the assumption being if they were crippled in body they were in mind also. Such prejudice was reinforced in later literary works such as Shakespeare's *Richard III*, and Victor Hugo's *Hunchback of Notre Dame*. Alternatively, the attitude was one of ridicule; a hunchback was often chosen to be the jester of the Court. During the Reformation prejudice grew worse as deformity came to be seen as being emblematic of heavenly wrath. The first author to portray crippled children in a sympathetic light was the great English novelist Charles Dickens. By treating fictional characters such as 'Tiny Tim' with compassion rather than contempt Dickens drew the British public's attention to the way in which handicapped children were treated, and to the relationship between poverty and childhood disease. Thanks to Dickens the disabled child became the object of philanthropic works. He also helped to establish some of the first children's hospitals. And Charles Dickens was also aware of the benefits of exposing children to the sun. In *The Adventures of Nicholas Nickleby*, which was originally published in monthly instalments between March 1838 and September 1839, Dickens described a visit to the countryside and the sunburnt faces of the half-naked gypsy children living there:

> It is a pleasant thing to see that the sun has been there; to know that the air and light are on them every day… that the limbs of their girls are free, and that they are not crippled by distortions, imposing an unnatural and horrible penance upon their sex…

He may have gained this insight while making plans for the book in the summer of 1837 when on holiday at Broadstairs, on the Kent coast. Dickens was an enthusiastic walker and was in the habit of visiting institutions of all kinds in search of material for his writing. It is likely that his travels took him to the Royal Sea Bathing Hospital at Margate, which was four miles from where he was staying. Founded in 1791 by the Quaker physician and philanthropist Dr. John Lettsom, this is believed to be the oldest orthopaedic hospital in the world. Certainly, if Charles Dickens did go there he would have had a unique opportunity to witness the effects of sunlight on bone diseases. Dr. Lettsom set up the hospital so that in the summer poor children from London who were suffering from tuberculosis could be taken to the coast to profit from the therapeutic properties of seawater and fresh air. Here Dickens may have seen some of the benefits of sun exposure he wrote about. He clearly appreciated its worth far more than the members of the Medical Research Committee investigating rickets were to do 70 years later. But then, medicine is a conservative profession and once a theory becomes orthodoxy, such as the widely held belief that rickets was caused by a syphilitic infection, it can take a long time to dislodge. The mistaken opinions of eminent figures in the medical world on the subject of rickets counted for far more than clinical observation or anecdotal evidence of the kind provided by Charles Dickens and Dr. Palm. Also, research into the causes of the disease only really began in earnest during the early years of the 20th century when X-ray equipment became available, giving doctors the means with which to measure changes in skeletal deformities. Prior to this, rickets was of passing interest only. So it was not until 1921 that scientists proved the sun was involved. Drs. Alfred Hess and Lester Unger of Columbia University in New York, published a paper in the *Journal of the American Medical Association* in which they related that exposing children to sunlight cured them of rickets. By this time Dr. Hess and other scientists had found out that a traditional remedy, cod liver oil, could prevent and cure rickets too. Unfortunately, the disease continued to be seen by many as one of dietary deficiency rather than lack of sunlight. Indeed, even today, rickets is referred to as a nutritional disease in medical textbooks. But from its emergence in England during the Maunder Minimum, then through the Industrial Revolution and well into the 20th century, rickets was endemic simply because babies did not get enough sunlight.

Following the belated recognition in 1921 that the sun's rays could prevent and cure rickets, sunbathing was promoted as a form of preventive medicine. Babies learned to crawl in the sun and doctors encouraged parents to put their offspring out in it at every opportunity. Nurses began instructing mothers on the correct procedure for children's sun baths. Within a short time the sun's rays came to be regarded as a universal tonic which, given the events of the preceding 300 years, is understandable. However, once rickets had been eliminated, medical thinking changed again. Vitamin D was relegated to a minor position in the nutritional league table and the sun came to be seen as harmful. Today, in marked contrast to the 1920s, parents are told to keep babies under 12 months out of direct sunlight, to put sunscreen on older children and, if possible, avoid the sun altogether from mid-morning to mid-afternoon. Predictably, rickets is resurgent and vitamin D deficiency is a global health problem among infants, as it is among the elderly and other groups. Today, in Britain and North America the infants most affected by rickets are of African-American, Afro-Caribbean, or

Asian descent. Their dark skin acts as a natural sunscreen and limits the amount of vitamin D they can produce. But any child who is kept out of the sun and has been exclusively breastfed is at risk. Breast milk can be a poor source of vitamin D if the nursing mother has low levels of it.

Tuberculosis and Vitamin D Deficiency

Children who were patients at Dr. Lettsom's Sea Bathing Hospital went there because they had tuberculosis rather than rickets; although it can be difficult to distinguish between the two. Often referred to as 'TB' or 'consumption', tuberculosis is an infectious disease caused by the tubercle bacillus, which is also known as *Mycobacterium tuberculosis*. TB can affect any part of the body. It is most common in the lungs in adults; and occurs almost everywhere else in children including the bones, joints, lymph glands, intestines and other internal organs. The history of tuberculosis in England follows a similar trajectory to rickets. It was just as prevalent and inflicted just as much suffering, if not more and, as with rickets, it was only in the first half of the 20th century that strenuous efforts were made to eliminate it. Tuberculosis became rampant as the Industrial Revolution got under way and people crammed into cities and lived in poor housing where contagion easily spread. Some estimates suggest that in the 1840s tuberculosis claimed the lives of at least 1 in 5 people in England; more than cholera, typhus, typhoid fever, smallpox, diphtheria, dysentery and all the other illnesses of the time put together. Charles Dickens, in common with so many Victorians, had first-hand knowledge of the disease. Shortly after he had finished writing *Nicholas Nickleby* his sister Fanny gave birth to a son. Although initially healthy, his nephew gradually developed a deformed spine and died at the age of 9 years: Fanny died of tuberculosis the year before. The damage to the spine of Dickens's nephew is consistent with the skeletal form of tuberculosis. If he was killed by TB like his mother, then vitamin D deficiency may have played a part in his death, and that of others with the disease.

The prevalence of rickets in Victorian England would suggest that vitamin D deficiency was endemic across all age groups. This is quite likely given the limited opportunities for sunlight exposure. But was it a factor in the prevalence of tuberculosis? Medical historians are silent on the subject, but vitamin D in the form of cod liver oil was a traditional remedy for TB, and sunlight therapy cured some forms of it. Scientists have only recently begun to investigate whether vitamin D can increase resistance to the disease. Until 2005 there had never been a properly conducted clinical trial to see if vitamin D could prevent or treat tuberculosis although it has been known for some time that vitamin D deficiency is common among TB patients.

Tuberculosis is diagnosed when a sample of phlegm examined under a microscope proves positive for the disease. Patients who have bacteria visible in their sputum are admitted to hospital and given a combination of antibiotics. When their sputum is clear and they are less infectious they can continue their drug therapy at home, unless they are in the advanced stages of the disease. In temperate climates TB is more likely to occur in the spring months when vitamin D levels are lowest. However, researchers have yet to find out whether vitamin D deficiency predisposes individuals to TB, or whether it is simply a result of the infection, or whether the antibiotics taken to treat it induce a deficiency. Nevertheless, it is now beyond doubt that vitamin D boosts anti-TB immunity significantly. In 2006 an article published in *Science* showed that vitamin D is central to the biological process the body uses to fight tuberculosis. Also, in 2006 scientists in Indonesia reported that a daily dose of 10,000 International Units (IU) of vitamin D for 9 months cleared the sputum of tuberculosis patients.

No doubt vitamin D supplements will become an adjunct to conventional therapy. Vitamin D may even be given to prevent the spread of what is still a very common and deadly illness. Globally, one third of the population is infected with TB, and more people are dying of it in the world today than at any other time in history. There are about 8 million new cases each year and about 2 million deaths. In 2002 the World Health Organization estimated that by 2020, roughly 1,000 million people will be newly infected, over 150 million people will get sick, and 36 million will die of TB if controls are not improved. A further problem is that TB can become resistant to antibiotics. When this occurs patients need more complex drugs that have to be taken for longer than the standard six months. Resistance can develop to a single drug or to more than one. Multiple drug resistant TB is potentially life threatening and is expensive, both in terms of the types of drugs needed to treat it, and the need for long periods in hospital. There are high rates of multiple drug resistant TB in Asia, parts of Eastern Europe and countries of the former Soviet Union. Foreign travel and increasingly mobile populations make it impossible for any country to isolate itself from the disease. Lack of sunlight and low levels of vitamin D could have played a major, if largely unrecognised, part in the continuing rise of tuberculosis.

Risks and Benefits

For many years there have been concerted public health campaigns warning of the dangers of sunbathing. But it is clear that there has never been a thorough, independent assessment of the risks and benefits of avoiding the sun. Given the long and unfortunate history of vitamin D deficiency in Britain and elsewhere, such an oversight is all the more surprising. Recent public health policy has consistently underestimated the importance of the sun as the body's primary source of vitamin D and overlooked the fact that there is little vitamin D in the normal diet. In North America, Europe and Australia the recommended dietary intake of vitamin D is set at a level that assumes that most of the population get enough casual exposure to sunlight to meet their vitamin D requirements. Unfortunately, the commonly used RDA (recommended daily allowance) for adults in Europe – 200 International Units a day – is inadequate as it is based on the amount needed to prevent rickets in children. The often-repeated assertion that casual exposure to the sun provides significant amounts of vitamin D and that prolonged exposure confers no further benefits is contrary to the facts. So too is the assumption that vitamin D generated in the summer is enough to last through the winter. It is not at northerly latitudes. During the winter months, when none is generated in human skin due to an absence of strong sunlight, the optimal intake of vitamin D may be 1,000 IU a day, if not more. Anyone who avoids the sun in the summer, and covers up when they do go out in it, will have low levels of vitamin D unless they take supplements. A study published in 2002 in the *Medical Journal of Australia* showed that vitamin D deficiency affects nearly one-in-four Australian women; in fact, vitamin D deficiency is now such a concern that there has been a change in public health policy: Australians are now advised to go out in the sun rather than avoid it. In 2005, a working group comprising the Australian and New Zealand Bone and Mineral Society, the Endocrine Society of Australia and Osteoporosis Australia concluded that it is a fallacy that Australians receive adequate vitamin D from casual exposure to sunlight. That the Australians struggle to maintain adequate levels of vitamin D throughout the year unless they actively seek sunlight should serve as a warning to us all.

While there is no doubt the incidence of skin cancers has risen over the last few decades in Australia and elsewhere, the exact nature of the relationship between sunlight and the most dangerous form – malignant melanoma – is unclear. Melanomas account for less than 10 per cent of all skin cancers, most of which are relatively benign. They commonly arise on parts of the body not much exposed to the sun, such as the soles of the feet, the back of the legs and buttocks. They can develop on skin that has not been exposed to the sun, and in internal organs, and melanomas are less common amongst people in outdoor occupations than those who work indoors. Regular, moderate exposure to sunlight offers some protection from the disease. The results of a study published in the *Journal of the National Cancer Institute* in 2005 shows that people who are in the early stages of melanoma are less likely to die of it if, in the past, they've spent a lot of time in the sun. Intermittent sunburn, particularly among youngsters who are susceptible to burning, is considered to be a risk factor. But melanoma mainly occurs in people who are genetically predisposed to the disease, have a fair complexion and pale eyes, or who have large numbers of moles on their skin. Also, there is evidence that some of our current problems with skin cancer and premature ageing stem from nutritional deficiencies. The proportion of fat in our food, together with the vitamin and mineral content can influence the way our skin responds to sunlight. And there is certainly no evidence that the increase in melanoma rates in recent years is linked to the 'hole' in the ozone layer.

Sun exposure in childhood is now believed to protect against diabetes, multiple sclerosis and prostate cancer in later life, all of which are much more common than malignant melanoma. Sunlight and exercise in childhood and adolescence build strong bones and this, in turn, helps prevent fractures and osteoporosis in old age. Staying out of the sun at a time of rapid bone growth and mineralization is a potentially dangerous thing to do. Low vitamin D levels during pregnancy can also harm children's growth. It can be a predisposing factor for the future development of a number of diseases, including diseases of the immune system, such as type 1 diabetes. A study published in the *The Lancet* in 2006 examined the vitamin D status of women in the final month of pregnancy living in the south-east of England. This is the sunniest part of the country, yet 50 per cent did not have adequate vitamin D levels.

Sunlight and Heart Disease

According to the World Health Organization, there are about 60,000 deaths annually from the ill-effects of sun exposure. By contrast, heart disease and stroke kill some 17 million people each year, and account for almost one-third of all deaths globally. In Britain, about 50,000 people a year develop skin cancers. Most are minor lesions that pose little threat to health and can be removed. In 2003, skin cancer claimed 2,280 lives, of which 1,770 were due malignant melanoma. How many of these deaths were directly attributable to sunburn and sunbathing is debatable, but in the same year cardiovascular disease killed more than 245,000 people and accounted for 40 per cent of all deaths. In crude terms the chances of someone dying of a heart attack in Britain is about 100 times greater than of dying of malignant melanoma. According to the British Heart Foundation, nearly half of all deaths from coronary heart disease in Britain are due to raised cholesterol levels. Whether cholesterol on its own will cause heart disease is questionable, but it has been known for more than half a century that exposure to ultraviolet radiation will lower blood cholesterol levels. A report from the 1953 meeting of the American Society for the Study of Arteriosclerosis describes how patients with hypertension and related circulatory problems who were exposed to UV radiation experienced an almost 13 per cent decrease in serum cholesterol levels.

High blood pressure is a major contributing factor to coronary heart disease. Scientists knew in the 1930s that exposure to UVB radiation will lower blood pressure in normal individuals and can have an even more pronounced effect on individuals with hypertension. Several studies strongly suggest that vitamin D has protective effects on the heart itself and may prevent the atherosclerosis that often leads to heart failure. Vitamin D improves muscular function, reduces blood pressure and the risks of developing juvenile diabetes, each of which is related to heart disease. It also increases the body's natural anti-inflammatory response and may suppress vascular calcification. Some of the strongest evidence that vitamin D deficiency is a risk factor for heart disease was published in the *Journal of the American College of Cardiology* in January 2003. In the first study of its kind in humans, cardiac patients and healthy volunteers were measured for levels of vitamin D, vitamin D metabolites and a hormone called n-terminal pro-atrial natriuretic peptide (ANP). A high blood level of ANP is a reliable indicator of cardiac failure, even in early stages, when the disease hardly shows any symptoms. In patients with chronic heart failure, vitamin D blood levels were as much as 50 per cent lower than those in the control group. The level of ANP, by contrast, had increased to more than twice the normal level in the cardiac patients. The severity of the disease was also correlated with the extent of vitamin D deficiency. Animal and in vitro studies suggest that vitamin D has the beneficial effect of reducing the production of ANP. It is also known that chicks with vitamin D deficiency develop heart failure, which improves when vitamin D is added to their feed.

Studies also show that more people die of heart attacks in the winter than in the rest of the year and deaths from heart disease are more common in populations living further from the equator. In addition to heart disease, vitamin D deficiency is present in most cases of acute stroke and may even precede one, according to research conducted at Addenbrooke's Hospital and published in the journal *Stroke* in 2006. One might reasonably assume from all this that more sunlight means better cardiovascular health. The balance of probability would suggest so. However, much of the evidence reviewed above could be dismissed as speculative and inconclusive. One reason for this is that full-scale clinical trials of vitamin D on heart disease and other leading causes of death have not been funded. Yet as the unfortunate history of rickets suggests, ignoring evidence of this kind until a definitive study is published can be damaging and costly. Cardiovascular disease is the leading cause of death worldwide and the reasons for this are still not understood. Vitamin D deficiency may be an important if largely ignored factor. Current estimates suggest that between 40 to 60 per cent of Europeans and North Americans are seasonally or chronically deficient in vitamin D. In all about 1 billion people worldwide may have inadequate levels in their bodies to prevent heart and other diseases. So even if exposure to UV radiation offers only modest protection it could result in a large reduction in mortality – far more than the number of skin cancer deaths each year. Health campaigns advocating sun avoidance, far from saving lives, may have had precisely the opposite effect. The history of public health is of well-intentioned initiatives that have sometimes had unforeseen and adverse outcomes. For the last 20 years medical experts have been telling us that ultraviolet radiation is harmful and advocated sun avoidance, and the use of sunscreens, without any supporting evidence that this will save lives. As soon as summer approaches this message is repeated in the media, with little regard to the fact that sunlight is the major source of vitamin D in the body, or that sunscreens can cut our ability to make vitamin D by 90 per cent.

Sunlight and Internal Cancers

As long ago as the 1930s doctors advocated sunbathing as a way of preventing cancer. Research by Dr. Sigismund Peller of Johns Hopkins University, published in the *Lancet* and in the *American Journal of Medical Science* in 1936, showed the high levels of sun exposure that sailors in the US Navy got in the course of their duties significantly reduced their risk of developing internal cancers. The benefits greatly outweighed the risks of skin cancer. In a similar manner to Dr. Palm's paper of 1890 on rickets, Dr. Peller's findings were ignored.

In 2006 in the *American Journal of Public Health,* Professor Cedric Garland and colleagues presented a review of all the papers published between 1966 and 2004 that examined the relationship between blood levels of vitamin D and cancer. This included 30 investigations of colon cancer, 26 of prostate cancer, 13 of breast cancer, and seven of ovarian cancer. It showed that the risk of developing some of these cancers could be cut by 50 per cent if vitamin D levels were kept high enough. To cite just one example, studies show that men who sunbathe, have holidays in sunny climates and have a history of sunburn have a better chance of avoiding prostate cancer than those who do not. Sunlight and vitamin D have also been shown to improve the prognosis of people who already have cancer. Research published by Professor Johan Moan and his colleagues at the Institute for Cancer Research in Oslo, Norway shows that summer sun improves survival for several forms of cancer, including breast, colon, prostate, lung cancer and lymphomas. The risk of a Norwegian dying of cancer within three years of diagnosis is reduced by as much as 50 per cent if they begin treatment in the summer and autumn rather than in the winter and spring.

The social costs and the economic burden of ignoring the link between sunlight and major cancers are large. According to one estimate, published in *Photochemistry and Photobiology* in 2005, some 50,000 to 63,000 individuals in the United States, and 19,000 to 25,000 in Britain die prematurely from cancer annually due to insufficient vitamin D. The cost to the U.S. economy of vitamin D insufficiency was put at $40–56 billion in 2004. By contrast, the economic burden of treating skin cancers and cataracts was put at $6 to 7 billion. Then there is the economic burden and premature loss of life associated with cardiovascular disease, multiple sclerosis, diabetes and osteoporosis to consider. These could be even higher than those for cancer.

We may be about to see a major reversal of public health policy, as it seems the extent of vitamin D deficiency among the general population and the death and disability this causes is finally being recognized. However, dermatologists and health policymakers would rather solve the problem with supplements than sunlight. Having spent so much time and effort trying to convince the general public that UV radiation is fundamentally harmful and confers no health benefits, this is understandable, if misguided. Taken in large quantities vitamin D is toxic. Unfortunately, the upper and lower limits of consumption for health are not known. As with sunlight, the amount needed may differ markedly from person to person depending on their age, state of health and constitution.

Sunlight or Supplements?

The great advantage of going out in the sun to get vitamin D is that it is impossible to produce too much for the body to cope with. It makes what it needs and then stores the surplus for periods when sunlight is unavailable. Full-body sunbathing for long enough to just start to turn skin pink will produce 10,000 to 20,000 IU of vitamin D, equivalent to 50 or more teaspoons of cod liver oil. Combining sunlight with supplements is not advisable because of the potential risk of toxicity. Also supplements such as cod-liver oil and multivitamin tablets contain vitamin A which in excessive amounts has been linked to osteoporosis and birth defects. Capsules containing 1000 IU of vitamin D3 are an inexpensive way of maintaining acceptable levels. But these are not available to buy over the counter in Britain as they are in other countries.

Vitamin D deficiency is insidious and notoriously difficult to diagnose. The symptoms can include muscle weakness, muscle and bone pain, fractures, loss of balance, gum disease, disrupted sleep, deafness and depression. The only way to gauge vitamin D levels in the body is to have a blood test although these are not always a reliable indicator. Regular, moderate exposure to the sun has many health benefits. And it produces copious amounts of vitamin D at safe levels.

Some groups are at higher risk of deficiency, including the housebound, the elderly who make vitamin D less efficiently than younger people, and those who cover up for religious or cultural reasons. People with dark skin, whose pigment blocks the absorption of UV radiation, are at particular risk if they live in temperate regions. They need about six to ten times as much sunlight to synthesize vitamin D as someone with very pale skin. There are people who should not go out in strong sunlight because of existing medical conditions, or because the drugs they are taking increase their sensitivity to it. Medicines that may cause adverse reactions include tranquillizers, painkillers, statins, diuretics, antibiotics, antifungal agents, oral contraceptives, immuno-suppressants, drugs for heart disease, hypertension, diarrhoea and epilepsy, and hormone replacement therapy. For those who do wish to sunbathe for health, there is one further obstacle to overcome. It can be difficult to do so in an urban environment for reasons that will be explained in Chapter 6.

Chapter 5
Superbugs and the Sun

The art of healing has changed dramatically down the centuries. As diseases that were major killers became quiescent, and others emerged to take their place, established procedures were rendered obsolete. Treatments that were once considered to be the best that medicine could offer were viewed with disdain, or worse. In addition, the wonder drugs of yesteryear have often proved to be harmful, or highly addictive, or both. Medicine moves on, but the diseases of the past never go away entirely and can reappear in new and more threatening forms. Smallpox, one of the most pestilent of all infectious diseases was eradicated in the 1980s – or so it seemed before bioterrorists became interested in it. Similarly tuberculosis was once considered beaten; but East London is now referred to as the TB capital of the Western world. For some of us the reemergence of these diseases stirs up half-forgotten memories of the medicine of a bygone era: of nurses wheeling bed-ridden patients onto the balcony of a tuberculosis sanatorium; or of relatives confined to the local fever hospital until they were no longer infectious. Occasionally the medicine of the past proves to be valid. The humble leech has returned to the operating theatre, and maggots are being used to clean up septic wounds and ulcers. But the sanatorium and the fever hospital have rather less to offer us. Or do they?

Over the past half-century, thanks to antibiotics, bacterial infections have been amenable to treatment. And it is fair to say that people have become rather more complacent about infectious diseases than they would have been say 50 or a 100 years ago. One consequence of this more relaxed attitude to infection is that there has been less emphasis on fresh air, light and cleanliness in hospitals than there was during the pre-antibiotic era. Unfortunately, the widespread and often indiscriminate use of antibiotics has reduced their potency and as a result, infectious diseases are becoming increasingly difficult and costly to treat. Strains of *Staphylococcus aureus* resistant to the antibiotic methicillin are endemic in hospitals and are increasing in non-hospital settings. Meanwhile hospital infections, whether from bacteria, viruses or fungi, are becoming more common. About 10 per cent of patients admitted to British hospitals acquire an infection during their stay, and the risk for a hospital-acquired infection has risen steadily in recent decades for several reasons. A higher proportion of patients are susceptible to infection because of the procedures they undergo, their advanced age, or the drugs they are given. The strains responsible for most infections in British hospitals are well-adapted to spreading between patients. And hygiene and cleanliness are certainly not what they once were.

So here is a simple experiment to show how much more important sunlight is in preventing infections than either skylight or artificial light. Go into a room that is sunlit. Close the curtains and turn on the lights. Then pick up an old cushion or pillow and beat it. Now turn off the lights and open the curtains so that a strong beam of sunlight enters the room. Beat the cushion again and see what happens. There should be a marked difference in the amount of dust that is visible coming off the cushion. Sunlight aids the perception of dust and dirt far more than either skylight or electric lighting, which is distinct advantage when cleaning a room. But more importantly, sunlight kills bacteria and viruses and will do so through glass. Most of the dust in buildings is human in origin. The surface of our skin is composed of microscopic scales and we lose and replace an entire layer of these skin cells about every four days. They part company with the body as we move, or when standing still in a state of undress. Then, having parted from us they fall to the floor or other horizontal surfaces, only to be resuspended by activities such as bed-changing, sweeping-up, the opening and closing of doors and windows, or the beating of cushions. Although not dangerous in themselves, skin cells can act as 'rafts' for some unpleasant and potentially lethal bacteria and viruses.

Dust has been recognized as a vehicle of infection for years, but a preoccupation with other theories of infection has sometimes obscured its true importance. Indeed, the idea that respiratory diseases can be passed from person-to-person by any means other than direct contact has swung back and forth over the years, from extremes of belief to extremes of disbelief. One of Rome's more distinguished doctors, Galen, wrote in the 2nd century AD that:

> ... when there is a common disease with many sufferers, one
> can refer it to a single common cause, the air.

Yet, eminent opinion has often held that respiratory infections are not passed in the air; nor even that they are contagious. The classic example of this is tuberculosis. For centuries doctors thought tuberculosis was a non-infectious, incurable disease that was either hereditary, or caused by a weak constitution, inflammation, or moral turpitude. In 1882, the German bacteriologist Robert Koch (1843–1910) proved otherwise having isolated the bacillus that caused the disease; but it was to some time before the infectious nature of tuberculosis was recognised in scientific circles, or by the general public. Gradually people became aware that they could catch tuberculosis from others if they breathed the same air, especially that found in dark, confined spaces.

When someone with active tuberculosis talks, coughs or sneezes they spray an aerosol of tiny droplets of mucus and saliva containing the bacillus. An infected person who coughs or sneezes violently will release thousands of these droplets into their immediate environment. Larger droplets quickly fall to the ground where they can land on dust particles, while smaller ones rapidly evaporate and decrease in size. In poorly ventilated areas these small droplets, or nucleii, can remain suspended in the air for several hours; or they can move with airflows and travel over long distances through buildings. The organisms in these droplet nucleii remain potentially infectious until they die. The tubercle bacillus is particularly resilient and, given the right conditions, can survive for months. Most of the work on its viability, or longevity, under room conditions was done in the years before the First World War. In 1904 a scientist successfully infected guinea pigs with the dust from a room six weeks after the death of its occupant. Another study showed that sputum folded in a handkerchief or blanket was still infectious after 70 days. Other pathogens display similar longevity and an attachment to dust. During the 1930s the attention of bacteriologists turned to dust-borne streptococcal infections in hospitals. These were thought to be to be responsible for prolonged epidemics of scarlet fever amongst patients. Scarlet fever used to be so common that hospital wards were reserved just for patients with the disease. Today it is not, although streptococcal infections can be just as dangerous as they were then, resulting in tonsillitis, pharyngitis, wound infections, abscesses, and occasionally pneumonia. When antibiotics were introduced in the 1950s infections such as these were becoming less common, thanks to improvements in housing and general living standards; tuberculosis was no longer the threat it had been and smallpox was all but eliminated. Fifty years later, TB has returned in new, more dangerous forms and rather more attention is being paid to it. The same applies to *staphylococcus aureus*. The number of infections and deaths from MRSA in British hospitals has become notorious.

The Sunlit Sanatorium

Much debate surrounds the control of MRSA infection. While the basis for this is thought to be hand washing, only about 40 per cent of infections are attributable to direct contact by medical staff. As to the rest, relatively little research work has been undertaken on the airborne transmission of *Staphylococcus aureus,* or any other bacteria and viruses, whether by droplet nucleii or dust. The dangers posed by airborne microbes in hospitals have been taken rather less seriously in recent years than they should have been. The part played by sunlight in reducing them has been ignored; and not for the first time. Florence Nightingale wrote about the dangers of dark rooms and of the purifying effect of direct sunlight on room air in her *Notes on Nursing* in 1860. At the time there was no scientific support for the idea, but in 1877 Downes and Blunt reported to the Royal Society that light, and especially sunlight, killed bacteria and could do so having passed through glass. Their work vindicated Florence Nightingale and prompted scientists to examine the effects of exposing bacteria to the sun's rays. Within a few years sunlight proved to be lethal to anthrax, tuberculosis and all manner of potentially harmful microorganisms. It was not long before sunlight was being hailed as 'nature's disinfectant' and an important weapon in the fight against infectious disease. Hospitals and sanatoriums were built with large south-facing windows to admit direct sunlight and prevent the spread of tuberculosis and other pathogens. In the years before antibiotics became widely available sunlit rooms were held to be hygienic, while those that did not admit the sun's rays were not. As the author of a book on sanatorium design, published in 1903, noted:

> *... every room occupied or visited by patients should be flooded by sunlight whenever possible, because, of all disinfectants, sunlight has been shown to be the most powerful.*

Today, in marked contrast, the germicidal properties of sunlight are not considered when buildings are being planned. One hospital design guide, published in 2001, even states that windows are not directly an infection control issue. Contemporary scientific evidence that sunlight can kill bacteria in hospital wards is very hard to find. One might reasonably assume that following Downes and Blunt's discovery, and the enthusiasm for sunlight as 'nature's disinfectant' that followed it, there would be a wealth of information on the subject. In fact, there is little. One reason for the dearth of scientific evidence is that over time the contact theory became a fashionable explanation for the spread of respiratory infection. With it came the implied exclusion of the air as a vehicle for the the spread of disease. And if the airborne route was of no consequence then neither was sunlight. Another possible reason for the absence of published data on sunlight's germicidal properties was the discovery that ultraviolet radiation in the invisible region of the solar spectrum was more lethal for bacteria than the visible portion. Scientists soon turned their attention to ultraviolet rays from lamps and away from sunlight once they realised the former were more potent. Fortunately, there are a few studies from the 1940s, which clearly show that sunlight through a window can rapidly kill bacteria and that sunlit wards have fewer bacteria in them than dark wards. Then, as now, it was becoming obvious that respiratory infections could not be explained by the contact theory alone, and that room environment might play a role in such infections.

Between 1941 and 1942, Dr. Leon Buchbinder and a team of investigators at Columbia University in New York, demonstrated that in the absence of light *streptococci* could survive with practically undiminished virulence for long periods indoors. They also confirmed something that Downes and Blunt suspected in 1877 but had been unable to prove, that the blue portion of the visible spectrum is the most germicidal. Tests showed that the lethal power of skylight through glass was significant. Its capacity to kill bacteria varied with its spectral distribution and intensity. Light from blue skies was the most effective while that of very cloudy skies the least. Direct sunlight, as might be expected, was much more lethal than daylight. The median survival time (or the time necessary for 50 per cent killing) of the alpha strain of *haemolytic streptococci* was about 5 minutes in the sun compared to more than an hour for diffuse daylight. The stronger the sunlight the more lethal it became. Surprisingly, they found the potency of sunlight per unit of intensity to be less than that of diffuse daylight; probably because there is more blue light in skylight than sunlight. They also examined the bactericidal effect of artificial light, as emitted by 15-watt tubular fluorescent lamps. These had little value as disinfecting agents because their output was so low.

By 1944 researchers in Britain had also begun to explore the impact of light and dark on *haemolytic streptococci* as part of a project to find out how far dust was responsible for the cross-infection of wounds in surgical wards. Thanks to the Second World War, there were plenty of opportunities for research. In contrast to America, where the direct contact theory was being challenged, in Britain the 'droplet' theory of infection was in the ascendant. It appears that for different reasons both countries were not giving dust its due. To the evident surprise of those involved in the British research, dust samples taken in some hospital wards were so virulent that they could easily have caused all the accidental infections recorded. In dark wards the bacterium flourished, while in well-lit wards it did not. Dark corners in infected wards were always more liable to yield dust containing *haemolytic streptococci* than more open situations. In one ward a dark recess beneath a bookcase was repeatedly sampled and it never failed to yield *streptococci*, yet dust on or close to windows never contained any. Again, as in the American study, *haemolytic streptococci* died most rapidly in direct sunlight in spite of this having to pass through two layers of glass: a window-pane and then a petri dish. Diffuse daylight from a north window was also lethal within 13 days or fewer, whereas in a dark cupboard in the same room, and thus under identical conditions apart from light, *streptococci* survived for many weeks. One strain of *haemolytic streptococci* in naturally infected dust survived in the dark, at room temperature, for 195 days. These findings were published in the *British Medical Journal* in 1944, and they appear to be the last of their kind.

Sunlight and Water

While the solar disinfection of buildings has not been of interest to scientists since then, the disinfection of water with sunlight has. Clean drinking water is a rare commodity in many developing countries, especially in rural areas. Every day, about 10,000 people die unnecessarily from diarrhoeal diseases. Many, if not most of these are children. Much of the water that is available to them carries bacteria and other pathogens and must be disinfected to make it safe. Conventional methods such as boiling or adding chlorine compounds can be expensive and time-consuming. Often there is little fuel available for boiling water, and it can be difficult to get hold of chlorine. There is another way of providing safe drinking water which is both cheap and highly effective. Put the water in a glass or plastic bottle, or a clear plastic bag, and leave it in direct sunlight for about eight hours. This simple measure will greatly reduce the risk of diarrhoea and cholera. The biocidal effect of solar disinfection is increased if the water heats up in the sun: a strong synergistic effect occurs at temperatures above 113°F, or 45°C. However, research into solar disinfection in buildings shows that it is the sun's light and not its heat that is responsible for killing bacteria so effectively.

Seasons and Infections

One of the observations made by Dr. Buchbinder during his work at Columbia University was that there were seasonal variations in the bactericidal effectiveness of skylight and sunlight. The killing action of each is proportional to their intensity, which suggested to him that their lethality might be greater in the spring and summer, when more solar energy is available, than in the autumn and winter. This cast new light on the possible relation of solar energy to the rise and fall of epidemics, a subject that has puzzled scientists for generations. For example, during the 1930s there were many outbreaks of streptococcal infections in British schools and, when a Medical Research Committee investigated them, one thing that became apparent was a marked seasonality:

> The dangerous periods are the Christmas and Lent terms in which the majority of streptococcal outbreaks have occurred; in only two instances has the appearance of a new epidemic strain been observed during the summer term, which together with the summer vacation appears to be a barrier to the extension of types already present.

Why the human population is so vulnerable to influenza, measles, pneumonia and other respiratory infections in the winter months, but relatively immune for the rest of the year remains a mystery. For example, influenza rates drop by more than 90 per cent for nine months of the year. This annual seasonal pattern has often been remarked on but never satisfactorily explained. Scientists have attributed it to changes in the prevalence or virulence of pathogens; or changes in atmospheric conditions; or the behaviour of the host population who tend to congregate indoors during the winter months. A confusing picture is made more so because the pathogens that cause these infections are present throughout the year, although for most of the time there are few accompanying epidemics.

When influenza pandemics occur they do so simultaneously in widely separated parts of the world. The lethal Spanish flu pandemic of 1918–19 killed more people than all the battles of the First World War. It was first detected *on the same day* in Boston and Bombay. Influenza gets its name from an Italian mediaeval Latin word meaning 'influenced by cosmic events'. In 1978 a possible connection between sunspot activity and the timing of influenza epidemics was suggested in *Nature* by Dr. Edgar Hope-Simpson (1908–2003), who was one of the world's great epidemiologists. He noted that sunspot activity and influenza pandemics both appear to occur in cycles of approximately 11 years. Hope-Simpson also observed that north of the tropic of Cancer and south of Capricorn epidemics usually break out in the winter, in parts of the globe that are most distant from the sun, six months after the time of maximum sunlight. He concluded from this that infection with the influenza virus depends on variations in solar radiation. People are more likely to get flu in the winter because lack of sunlight activates the virus.

In 2001, scientists at the Centers for Disease Control and Prevention in Atlanta published an article in the journal *Emerging Infectious Diseases* in which they also suggested that our susceptibility to influenza and other infections may be mediated by the sun and the way it influences our resistance to disease. Seasonal patterns of respiratory infections around the world could be due to seasonal changes in the immunity of the people who get them. This is consistent with the observation that there are seasonal variations in cancer, heart attacks and other apparently noninfectious conditions. So although the influenza virus and other pathogens are present year-round, it seems it is only when natural light levels fall that the susceptibility of the population increases enough to sustain flu epidemics. Of course, there may be two factors at work here: less sunlight in the winter means bacteria and viruses become more virulent while we become more vulnerable to them. This increased susceptibility may be due to low levels of serotonin, or too much melatonin during the day or, most likely, a decline in vitamin D levels.

Lack of sunlight may be responsible for the coughs, colds and influenza and other infections that many of us fall prey to in the winter. It is worth bearing in mind the health and economic costs of respiratory infections are enormous. A recent example that illustrates the point is the severe acute respiratory syndrome (SARS) virus, which has the distinction of being the first new disease of the 21st century. In 2003 this caused many deaths, widespread panic and economic losses of more than $40 billion before apparently coming under control. There is always the possibility that SARS could re-emerge or that we have to deal with an influenza pandemic or, however remote, a bioterrorist attack. Unfortunately, modern buildings are not arranged to prevent the spread of virulent infections. Indeed, there are strong incentives to design new and retrofit old buildings to lessen the contribution of fresh outdoor air to indoor ventilation and to keep out the sun. Florence Nightingale remarked that: *'True nursing ignores infection, except to prevent it'.* Her views on architecture were just as forthright, particularly where sunlight and fresh air were concerned.

Florence Nightingale and the Pavilion Ward

By the 1850s, Florence Nightingale had become an expert on nursing and on hospital design. When she wrote *Notes on Nursing* and *Notes on Hospitals*, infectious diseases and especially childhood infections were rampant. She estimated that one in every seven children in England died within 12 months of birth and that in London two in every five children died before the age of five. They died of diphtheria, whooping cough, measles, scarlet fever, cholera, typhoid fever, smallpox, dysentery, pneumonia and a host of other illnesses. Florence Nightingale had seen all manner of pestilential illnesses at first hand in hospitals throughout Europe and had witnessed the enormous loss of life that they could inflict. During the Crimean War, thousands of British soldiers died of infections while under her care within the walls of the infamous Scutari hospital. One insight she gained from this was that the environment in which patients found themselves could contribute to their recovery, or it could hasten their demise. This was a novel idea in its day and to some extent it remains so. Miss Nightingale insisted that a hospital worthy of the name was for the benefit of one person alone – the patient. Then, as now, hospitals were arranged as much for the convenience of carers and managers as they were for the sick. For example, the results of a survey published in the journal *Building and Environment* in 1976 showed that while 91 per cent of hospital patients valued sunshine in their environment, 62 per cent of hospital staff considered sunshine to be a nuisance. If doctors and nurses are inconvenienced when working in sunlit spaces they are unlikely to insist on them for their patients.

Florence Nightingale believed the sun's rays purified the air and reduced the risk of cross-infection. Also, in marked contrast to some of the leading doctors of the day, she held that a view of the sky and especially sunlight was of the utmost importance to the sick. So much so that they should be able to see both without raising or turning in bed, and if they could see out of two windows instead of one so much the better. Morning sun and midday sun were of more benefit to them than the afternoon sun. Something else she insisted on was fresh air, and lots of it. The air within a hospital ward had to be as pure as the air outside, without chilling the patients. Air was not fresh if it was not warmed by the sun, nor was it safe if it came from anywhere other than an open window. In the 1850s the effect of poor ventilation on the sick and the well were not generally recognised. It was not unusual for medical staff to keep ward windows hermetically closed for fear of lowering the air temperature. But Miss Nightingale believed otherwise:

To attempt to keep a ward warm at the expense of making the
sick repeatedly breathe their own hot, humid, putrescing
atmosphere is a certain way to delay recovery and destroy life.

She had noticed from her experiences in the Crimea that patient mortality rates were much lower in temporary field hospitals than they were in large hospital buildings. So she became an advocate of the pavilion system, originally a French arrangement of separate ward units. The Nightingale ward, as it became known, ensured that air did not come from polluted sources such as corridors into which other wards were ventilated, or hallways, or closed courtyards. Florence Nightingale believed that corridors spread infection from one ward to another and was opposed to any form of mechanical ventilation because there was always the possibility that it might do the same. Patients in her wards slept next to open windows wrapped up warmly in bed with a hot-water bottle. If they were well enough to move about and could open and shut windows themselves then so much the better. A coal fire kept the ward warm and its chimney provided more ventilation. But Florence Nightingale maintained that no amount of air, pure or otherwise, could freshen a room or ward where the most scrupulous standards of hygiene were not maintained.

The curative effects of fresh air had been well known since the time of Hippocrates and Galen and were used by a few physicians in the 18th and 19th centuries. In 1840, Dr. George Boddington (1799–1882) published a famous essay on the treatment of tuberculosis of the lungs with cold air in what was to become known as the 'open-air method' of treating the disease. The pavilion ward and, later, the tuberculosis sanatorium were two of the first building types specifically designed to take advantage of the supposed recuperative properties of fresh air. Both could be thoroughly ventilated. However, neither type was arranged for sunlight therapy. The Nightingale ward was about 120 feet long and 30 feet wide and could accommodate between 20 and 30 beds. Although extensively glazed by the standards of the day, with a minimum of one window for every two beds, there was only one entrance. So there was no way of getting patients outside without much inconvenience to all concerned. Tuberculosis sanatoriums were designed to be sunlit in an attempt to kill bacteria, prevent infections spreading, and cheer up the patients. But facilities for sunbathing were not normally provided, as heliotherapy did not form part of the open-air regime. Photographs of open-air sanatoriums often show patients, in their beds, on balconies or verandas. Bedclothes cover them and there is no evidence of any attempt to expose their bodies to direct sunlight; as the following extract from an article in *The Lancet* of 1923 confirms:

*In the sanatorium treatment developed during the last 50
years, the action of direct sunlight plays no part, and no
provision is made for it in the majority of sanatoriums.*

When the first sanatoriums were built, sunlight was not thought to be therapeutic for tuberculosis of the lungs. And later, when doctors tried heliotherapy on pulmonary TB this proved to be potentially dangerous. Although good results were reported, it had to be carried out with the greatest care as too much sun exposure could result in haemorrhage, or a spread of the infection to other parts of the body with potentially fatal consequences. Institutions for the heliotherapy of rickets, war wounds and non-pulmonary tuberculosis were, on the other hand, designed so that sunlight could be clinically applied with the specific objective of tanning the patients to cure them. So in architectural terms it is often difficult to distinguish between open-air sanatoriums for pulmonary tuberculosis and heliotherapy clinics, as both were oriented for sunlight, but for different reasons. What the Nightingale ward, the tuberculosis sanatorium and the heliotherapy clinic all had in common was they were designed to make conditions indoors as close to those outdoors as possible. This was thought to both therapeutic and hygienic. There is some logic in this because the bacteria and viruses that cause infections in humans cannot tolerate sunlight or the temperature extremes that occur outdoors. It is only in the warm, humid and often dimly lit spaces where humans congregate that pathogens can survive and make airborne excursions from one host to the next.

When antibiotics became available the emphasis shifted from putting hospital patients in wards that supported healing to ones that provided a more comfortable environment for hospital patients and staff. The idea that a building, in itself, could be therapeutic became unfashionable. Standards of hygiene fell, and sunlight and fresh air were no longer considered important. So much so that wards were built without windows at all. Fifty years later the pendulum is starting to swing back. Deprivation of natural light is now recognised as contributing to increased stress and reduced immunity. Research in intensive care units strongly suggests that a lack of windows can have a damaging effect on patients and causes higher rates of depression, anxiety and post-operative delirium. Also, sleep deprivation is another stress factor that can interfere with recovery from disease, and light levels in wards are often too high at night as well as too low during the day. As we now live in the era of 'superbugs', avian flu and the SARS virus, a little more sunlight during the day and darkness at night could save many lives, and not just in hospitals.

Chapter 6
Overcoming Light Deprivation

Estate agents know the attractions of a sunny plot when they see one. Properties that get the sun are supposed to fetch higher prices and yield higher rents than those that do not. Yet, this is not reflected in the way buildings and cities are planned. The modern dwelling is not open to the sun and neither are our towns and cities for the simple reason that most of them don't point in the right direction. This is why the urban environment can be a serious impediment to sunlight and sunbathing. While some of our more conscientious designers do configure buildings to take advantage of the sun, most do not. In practice, it is the orientation of a city that usually determines the orientation of the buildings within it and not the architect. And it is the orientation of a city that dictates how much sunlight each dwelling gets. Usually the streets are laid out first and then the houses, shops and offices are put on them. So if the streets are not lined up for the sun then nothing else is. The estate agent's well-known mantra is 'location, location, location'. But where sunlight and health are concerned 'orientation, orientation, orientation' is everything. We will find out why, and examine the relationship between the city, the dwelling and the sun in a moment. But before doing so it might be useful to familiarise ourselves with the practice of phototherapy and, in particular, the medical use of sunlight. Many of the architects who designed for light and health at the beginning of the last century were familiar with the medicine of their day. They knew about sunlight therapy and sometimes worked alongside doctors who used the sun. So we'll start out on this path by looking at the findings of the first scientist to investigate the sun's healing powers.

Given all of the adverse publicity that sunbathing gets, and the lengths to which dermatologists will go to warn us of the dangers, it's ironic that the only dermatologist ever to be awarded the Nobel Prize for Medicine was a sunlight therapist. Professor Niels Finsen (1860–1904) almost single-handedly dragged light therapy back into the mainstream of western medicine at the beginning of the last century. Finsen was the first doctor to both use sunlight in clinical practice and study its effects scientifically. He began his research when he fell ill as a medical student. He suffered from anaemia and tiredness, and since he lived in a house facing north, he thought it might help if he received more sun than he was getting. He spent as much time as possible in sunlight and, as an enthusiastic medical man, was keen to know what benefits the sun gave.

The first problem Finsen faced when he began to research the subject was that there was nothing in his physiology textbooks that suggested that sunlight held any advantages at all. So from about 1888 onwards he found out all he could about it. He studied the behaviour of animals in the sun, and in particular the way they seek it out. His observations strengthened both his conviction that the sun had positive effects and his determination to find out what they were. Finsen's aim even at this early stage was to exploit the therapeutic properties of the sun in the form of sunbathing or artificial light baths. But he felt that it would be wrong to do so without first having a thorough understanding of them based on scientific research and definite facts, rather than speculation. Finsen spent the next 15 years trying to uncover what the sun's useful effects were. He failed to do so, but on the way made many discoveries about light and health and developed new ways of treating diseases. He devised a form of phototherapy for smallpox in 1893, and one for tuberculosis in 1895, for which he received the Nobel Prize. Despite these achievements and the recognition they gained him, Finsen regarded his work on smallpox and tuberculosis as side issues, distractions which drew him away from his elusive goal; the sun.

In Finsen's day scientists were still struggling to understand what light did to living organisms. In 1666, two hundred years before Finsen began his research, the English physicist Sir Isaac Newton (1642–1727) famously used a quartz prism to refract sunlight into the seven primary colours: red; orange; yellow; green; blue; indigo and violet. Each of these colours possesses three properties: the power to produce heat; light and chemical changes. Scientists knew that the red rays were the chief source of heat, that light had its greatest intensity in the yellow; and the violet rays were mainly chemical. But the visible spectrum represents only a small part of the sun's output. At each end there are the two much larger fields: the infra red and ultraviolet about which little was known. By exposing insects, tadpoles, salamanders and earthworms to the various parts of the solar spectrum, Finsen showed that it was only the blue, violet and ultraviolet rays that have a significant physiological effect. These 'actinic' or chemical rays provide most of the stimulus for biological processes. He found the red portion of the spectrum – the heat rays – had no effect, and the yellow portion of sunlight hardly any.

Red Light and Smallpox

In one simple yet elegant experiment Finsen placed twenty earthworms in an oblong box. He had made a lid for the box with a series of glasses of different colours arranged in order of the spectrum; red, yellow, green, blue. A few minutes after the lid was in place, all of the worms moved under the red glass. He turned the lid around so the blue replaced the red and, again, the worms moved to the red portion of the box. He repeated the experiment several times, and the result was always the same whether sunlight or skylight was used. Under red glass the worms lay quiet in a heap, but under blue glass they became agitated and then moved away. Finsen deduced from this that people suffering from smallpox, whose skin was acutely sensitive, would recover better in red light than in daylight. In 1893 he published a paper in which he put forward the theory that if smallpox patients were protected from blue, violet and ultraviolet radiation they would be spared the suppuration and scarring that normally follows infection. Although Finsen had never seen a case of smallpox he was aware that the worst scarring occurs on the face and hands, the parts of the body most exposed to daylight. He had also read of several cases where patients had been kept in total darkness and had recovered without the usual pockmarking and scarring. Finsen reasoned that patients in the early stages of the disease should be kept in red light, rather than in the dark. This would protect them from the 'chemical' rays just as effectively as total darkness with the added advantage that patients and medical staff would be able to see one other. Two months after his paper was published doctors in Norway put this theory to the test. Eight smallpox patients were kept in red light for the duration of their illness. The most painful stage of smallpox – the period of suppuration – did not occur, and there was no swelling or pitting of the skin and no temperature rise. Doctors elsewhere in Scandinavia and Europe tried Finsen's 'red-chamber' therapy. Although the results were often favourable, medical opinion was sharply divided on the subject.

Finsen then turned his attention to the blue end of the spectrum and its capacity to kill the tubercle bacillus. The sun's bactericidal properties were well known among the scientific community at this time. The French scientist Emile Duclaux, had written in 1885 that: *'sunlight is the best, cheapest and most universally applicable bactericidal agent we have.'* Finsen demonstrated that just like its physiological effects, the bactericidal action of sunlight is most marked in the blue, violet and ultraviolet rays. He showed that by concentrating sunlight, focusing it through lenses, its germ-killing action could be increased and that it could be used to kill bacteria on the skin. He also proved that light from a powerful carbon-arc lamp could do the same. Finsen also examined the causes of *erythema solare*, or sunburn. He conducted experiments in which he exposed himself to strong ultraviolet radiation from an electric arc-lamp. At the time, people still thought that it was the 'heat' of sun's rays that caused tanning but Finsen confirmed other scientists observations that it was the 'actinic' rays that caused it.

Tuberculosis and the Sun

In 1897 Finsen published a paper entitled *The Treatment of Lupus by Concentrated Chemical Rays,* which describes the methods and results he got from the tests he carried out from 1895 onwards. He discovered that concentrated ultraviolet light could clear up *Lupus Vulgaris,* a disease thought to be incurable. This is a particularly unpleasant form of tuberculosis that mainly affects the face. It is rarely fatal, but causes severe disfigurement. The only treatment available at the beginning of the last century was surgery, which involved cutting, scraping, or burning it away with acid and hot irons. This did not remove the seat of the infection and made the disfigurement even worse. Finsen reasoned that Lupus would be responsive to exposure to concentrated ultraviolet light, as the tubercle bacillus is superficial in this form of the disease, and he thought the light could penetrate and kill it. He also felt the stimulus of light would assist recovery. This was the work that gained Finsen the Nobel Prize, but he also carried out preliminary research into the effects of sunbathing on tuberculosis of the bones joints and skin; and on pulmonary tuberculosis.

Although Finsen failed in his search to uncover the secrets of the sun's healing properties before he died in 1904, he did inspire other doctors to use sunlight. One thing that they noticed when they started to practice heliotherapy was the importance of timing. Putting patients who were very ill with tuberculosis and war wounds in the sun just after dawn was often more beneficial than any other time of day. They also found that the best time of year to sunbathe was in the spring and early summer. Sunbathing in spring prepares the body for stronger sunlight later in the year, and makes good any shortage of vitamin D that may have developed over the preceding winter. Early morning is the best time to begin exposure of skin that is not used to sunlight, because the sun is just above the horizon and so there is less chance of burning than there is later in the day. A further advantage is that exposure to bright light early in the day has psychological benefits. Light therapy trials show bright light to be more effective for seasonal depression when given in the morning, rather than in the evening. And then there are the benefits of dawn simulation described in Chapter 3.

Heliotherapy and Modern Architecture

Historical evidence suggests that to get the best from sunlight we have to be able to see it rise. Not only that, but we need spaces where we can commune with it. Before the Industrial Revolution there were ample opportunities to do so but since then, thanks to our increasingly urbanized world, it can be difficult to find somewhere with early morning solar access. This is not a new problem: it was one doctors had to grapple with at the beginning of the last century when, thanks to Finsen, they rediscovered heliotherapy and wanted to heal tuberculosis and rickets with it. Many of their patients were bedridden and needed to be wheeled outside to get the sun on them. But few, if any, hospital wards were suitable for sunbathing, and so doctors had to improvise. They rearranged existing buildings; introducing measures which made sunlight therapy a practical proposition. These innovations were taken up by the leading architects of the day, and formed the basis for what became known as Modernism.

Dr. Auguste Rollier opened his first sunlight clinic in Leysin, in the Swiss Alps in 1903. Rollier developed a method of slow, careful tanning specifically for severely weakened patients who could not respond as well to sunlight as a healthy adult. Exposure was very gradual, and only increased by about five minutes each day. His first clinic was an old boarding house, which he converted to take 50 patients and to provide them with direct access to the sun. This involved extensive remodelling of the property. The windows were substantially enlarged; south-facing balconies created on the ground floor; and partition walls removed to create large dormitories. When Dr. Rollier took over the boarding house it already had second floor balconies. But these could not be made wide enough to hold the patients from the adjacent rooms. So he introduced an innovation; a large solarium on the roof where patients could sunbathe from morning to evening.

Rollier proposed 'Le Chalet', as his clinic became known, as a model for those wishing to start a practical and inexpensive sanatorium for sunlight therapy. It was here that Rollier achieved many of the cures that were to make his international reputation in the years that followed. The modifications he made to this seminal building may seem modest by today's standards but at the time they were revolutionary and it could be that they changed the course of western architecture. The origins of the Modern Movement are a matter of some discussion among architectural historians. Anyone engaged in a search for them could do worse than start with 'Le Chalet', as this was the first building to incorporate Modernism's key motifs: a roof-solarium; large south-facing windows; an open-plan interior; and balconies. Rollier was only too aware that much of the tuberculosis he saw at Leysin had its origins in poorly lit and badly ventilated housing. His views on the need for sunlight in fresh air dwellings are outlined in his book *Quarante Ans d'Héliothérapie,* and in the conclusion of a paper he wrote on heliotherapy in the *British Medical Journal* of 1922:

> *These elements should have a larger place given them, in daily life and in the city. Not only modern towns should be built on such hygienic principles, but also the home. Housing has played an immense part in the genesis of child and adult tuberculosis: the community bears the responsibility of the waste of human lives through insanitary houses.*

Orientation and Sanitation

Balconies, solaria and the rest are only of value if they are orientated correctly. Sunbathing is impractical in the shadow of a building. Similarly, hygiene and sanitation in and around buildings depends on judicious orientation to ensure access to the sun. It can be much more difficult to clean and maintain an outdoor space which gets little or no sunlight than one which is sunlit. Wall surfaces, especially brick and concrete walls absorb a large amount of moisture when it rains. This moisture quickly dries when exposed to sunlight, but is retained for along time in walls that do not get the sun. Dampness, with lack of sunlight, is a combination favourable to the growth of moulds, fungi and all manner of unpleasant micro-organisms. The World Health Organization favour solar design for this reason:

> *If no sunlight reaches the external environment around buildings, the dark outdoor spaces become dank and infested with undesirable flora and fauna. Biological decay is slowed and cleanliness deteriorates... Direct sunlight aids external sanitation... laundry dries more effectively and hygienically.*

Cold, damp housing is synonymous with poor health. People in poorly heated homes are more vulnerable to winter death than those living in well-heated homes. In warmer climates health problems can arise from pools of water near to buildings. Standing water that does not evaporate quickly can become colonised with mosquito larvae. When these hatch they can be vectors for malaria, dengue fever and other potentially fatal diseases. A dwelling that is arranged for health is carefully oriented towards the sun both for sunbathing and sanitation. To understand how best to achieve this we have to go back, yet again, to the beginning of the last century and look at the work of a pioneer in the field. The first man who studied the subject in detail was William Atkinson, an architect from Boston, Massachusetts who specialized in hospital design. When Mr. Atkinson was not building hospitals he was investigating how best to arrange them for the sun. He wrote in 1905 that: *'Unquestionably the first requisite of a hospital is abundance of sunlight'*. To this end William Atkinson found out how to ensure that the exterior wall surfaces and the ground around hospitals had the direct rays of the sun for as long a time as possible each day. He also made sure the patients in his wards benefited from sunlight too. He felt that the same principles should apply to residential properties. As he put it: *'If sunlight is essential for the recovery of the sick, is it not a still more powerful agent in the prevention of disease?'* Atkinson wrote and lectured widely in an attempt to improve architects' knowledge of what he considered to be a vital subject. He was concerned that many of the hospitals built in America at the time were not oriented correctly. Nor, indeed, were America's towns and cities.

Mr. Atkinson's Lesson

Figure 7 shows what William Atkinson called the 'first lesson' in orientation. It represents two buildings in Boston at a latitude of 42°. Both are square in plan. The first is aligned with the points of the compass, squarely with the meridian, and in the other the meridian passes through the diagonal. The north wall of the first building will get no sunlight at all for half the year, from the autumn equinox to the spring equinox.

In the second case all four walls of the building will get some sunlight during all four seasons of the year. Figure 7 is a 'shadow plan' of the two buildings from sunrise to sunset at the equinoxes. The sun rises in the east at about six o'clock, travels south and sets in the west at six o'clock.

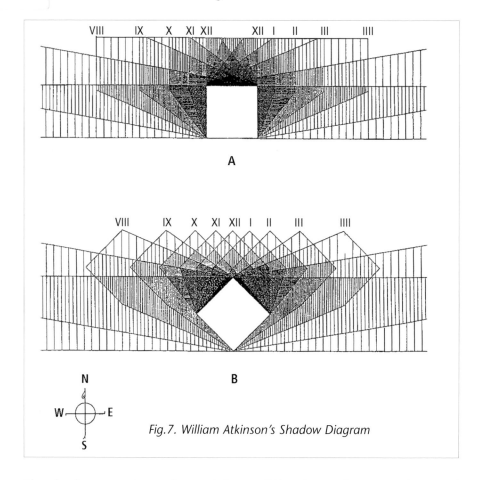

Fig.7. William Atkinson's Shadow Diagram

The shadows are drawn for each hour of the day and are superimposed one on top of another. The degree of blackness corresponds roughly to the length of time that a particular spot is in shadow from sunrise to sunset. Full black represents an area which is in sunlight for less than an hour. The first building has a triangle of shadow behind it, which is much larger than that of the second building. This shows that a square building placed in the latter position shades the ground around it much less than one placed in the position of the first one which has a 'dark side' for six months of the year. As Atkinson was aware, the traditional plan of a Swiss mountain chalet was a square building set on the diagonal to the meridian, with the living room placed at the southern apex. This is the healthiest and safest arrangement in areas of heavy snowfall, or anywhere else for that matter. In alpine regions it helps to keep walls clear of snow, and paths clear of ice. In milder climates it helps to keep buildings and their surroundings clean and dry.

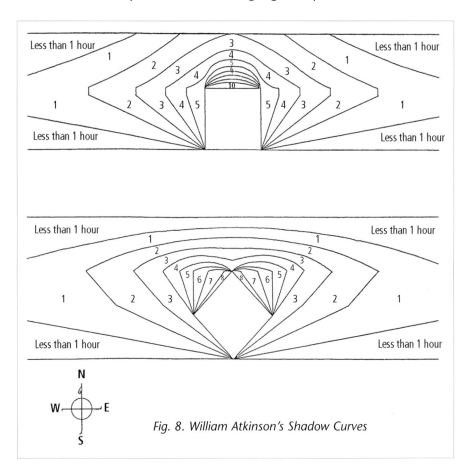

Fig. 8. William Atkinson's Shadow Curves

Atkinson also developed a means of representing shadows using curves rather than shading, by joining the intersections of various shadows. In Figure 8 one set of curves follows points which are in shadow for exactly one hour. The next joins a series of points in shadow for two hours, and so on. And so he traced the shadow curves of both buildings. The numerals indicate the number of hours during which each area is in shadow: that is, the areas marked 1 are in shadow from one to two hours: those marked 2 in shadow from two to three hours, and so on. A shadow diagram of any building can be drawn using the same method and it is a useful way to find out how potentially healthful it is.

The Sunny Side of the Street

William Atkinson used the same technique to show that there were marked seasonal differences in the amount of sunlight and shadow in streets depending on their orientation. In most American cities the streets are laid out on a north and south, east and west grid, squarely with the meridian. Atkinson held that this was a flawed approach. The best way to arrange a system of streets running at right angles to each other is to lay them out on the diagonals southeast-northwest and southwest-northeast just as it is with buildings.

One problem with the conventional grid pattern that runs east-west and north-south is that in the winter, when sunlight is at a premium, a street that runs east to west in a built-up area will be in shadow for much of the day. At noon the sun will be low in the southern sky so its rays will penetrate only a small distance down into it. Streets in built-up areas with this orientation remain dark and cold through the winter months. By contrast, in summer the sun comes down the street from the east in the morning and from the west in the afternoon, and by midday it is nearly overhead. So streets that run east-west get little shadow at midday in summer, and even less in the morning and afternoon. The east-west street is a street of extremes; too cold and dark in winter and too hot in summer.

A north-south street is sunny during the midday in winter but will be in shadow during the morning and afternoon. Although a north-south street gets more sunshine in the winter than any other alignment, at other times of the year a diagonal street is almost equal to it. The great disadvantage of the north-south street is that in the summer at midday, when the sun is at its strongest, there is no protective shadow. Contrast this with a grid of streets that runs southeast-northwest and southwest-northeast. At the height of summer there is shadow in every street during the day, except for the few minutes the sun shines down one or other diagonal street in the mid-morning and mid-afternoon. While there is plenty of shade in the summer, in the winter the streets are sunlit in the morning and remain so until well into the afternoon. At midday in the winter, when the sun is due south there are shadows in all the streets but, even so, more sunlight penetrates than if they were aligned east-west.

William Atkinson was by no means the first to recognise the superiority of streets aligned with the diagonals. As long ago as the 4th century B.C., Hippocrates alluded to it in his *'Airs, Waters, Places'* when he commented that cities facing the rising sun are more likely to be healthy than those with any other orientation. Yet cities oriented in this way are the exception and not the rule. The north-south, east-west grid predominates in the USA, and elsewhere, and there may be a valid reason for this. But as far as access to sunlight is concerned it is not the best arrangement. Dark streets have dark houses and dark houses are unhealthy.

The Solar City

The idea of the city as a sunlit Utopia has held the imagination of emperors, kings and philosophers for millennia. One of the first to be built was the handiwork of the Egyptian Pharaoh Akhenaten (1353–1337 BC) of the 18th Dynasty. Here was an entire city devoted to the worship of the sun, with its avenues laid out on a grid that runs roughly southeast-northwest and southwest-northeast. Called Akhetaten, or the 'Horizon of the Aten,' it stood in splendid isolation at a remote site on the banks of the Nile. Akhenaten built it far away from Egypt's two traditional capitals, Thebes and Memphis, at what is now the village of El Amarna. Dedicated to the Aten, or sun's disc, this city was where the 'heretic Pharaoh' and his Queen Nefertiti established a new monotheistic religion, rejecting the old Egyptian gods and their priesthood and venerating the life-giving powers of the sun. This new dispensation did not last long, however. When Akhenaten died the site was abandoned and within a generation of his reign the city was no more. His successor Tutankhamun restored Ra, Amun and the rest of the pantheon and moved Egypt's capital back to Memphis. Although Akhenaten's light revolution lasted for a mere 20 years or so, his vision of a solar paradise was to prove more enduring. There were to be other solar cities. The Greeks built them, not for religious purposes or those of health, but to save energy.

During the fifth century BC, the Greeks faced severe fuel shortages. Firewood was scarce and had to be imported. Archaeological evidence shows the ancient Greeks responded to this crisis by planning cities in Greece and Asia Minor to allow every homeowner access to sunlight during winter to warm their homes. The Greek author Aeschylus (525–456 BC) alludes to this in his play *Prometheus Bound.* He tells how the gift of fire, stolen from the Gods of Olympus, raised humanity from a state of servitude and wretchedness. Thanks to the generosity of Prometheus, people could live in brick-built dwellings warmed by the sun, whereas before they lived like '... *ants in sunless caves*'. The Greeks adopted the familiar grid or chequerboard pattern which ran east-west and north-south. Every home faced south to capture the winter sun throughout the day and provide shelter from the cold north winds. Although the Greeks' sun–gods, Apollo, Helios and Asklepius, were deities of health and healing, their solar cities were arranged to save energy and not prevent disease. Every house would have had a 'dark side'. Meanwhile, in ancient China solar planning evolved along similar lines. The streets of major cities were aligned with the points of the compass, with the main rooms of the houses facing south to capture the winter sun. The Romans had strict right-to-sunlight legislation but they did not plan their cities for sunlight as the Greeks and Chinese had. Designing for the sun was a matter for each citizen, not the state. Some cities, such as Pompeii, were laid out on the diagonal while others, such as neighbouring Herculanium, were not. And so it was that the solar city gradually disappeared from the European landscape.

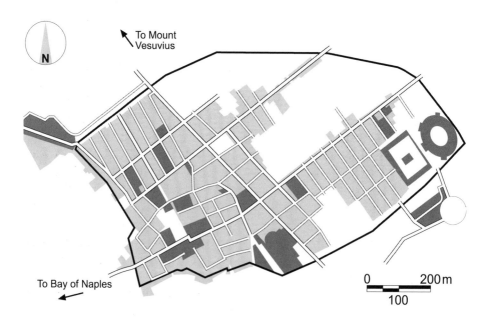

Fig. 9. Map of Roman Pompeii at a latitude of 40° 45', North.
Copyright: Current World Archaeology

Utopia means *nowhere* or *no-place* and so, strictly speaking, Akhenaten's solar city does not qualify as a Utopia because it existed. Europe's first imaginary solar city appeared in 1602, when an Italian monk Tomasso Campanella (1568–1639) published *The City of the Sun.* Campanella's Utopia has much in common with Akhetaten in that its inhabitants worshipped the sun as the image of God, and their leader is a high priest who conducts solar ceremonies. Architecturally however, things are different. The walls of this solar city form seven concentric circles around a central sun-temple and are named after the seven planets. There are four main streets and four gates that look toward the four points of the compass. Campanella's description of this idealised theocratic commune owes something to earlier Utopian texts, such as Plato's *Republic* and Sir Thomas More's original *Utopia* of 1516. The priest class who rule the City of the Sun are reminiscent of Plato's philosopher-kings. For Plato the sun represented the highest ideal or ultimate 'good' in much the same way as it had for Akhenaten and later did for Campanella. However, the next solar city to appear in European literature had no such antecedents and was a far more practical proposition. This was the work of one of the great sanatarians of the Victorian era.

Dr. Benjamin Ward Richardson (1828–1896) was the founder and editor of the *Journal of Public Health and Sanitary Review,* which was the first periodical of its kind. Dr. Ward Richardson was a disciple of Sir Edwin Chadwick (1800–1890) who organized the campaign to rid towns and cities of the filth and squalor that accompanied the Industrial Revolution. Chadwick's efforts resulted in the great Public Health Act of 1875. It was also in 1875 that Dr. Ward Richardson gave an address to his fellow sanatarians at the annual meeting of the Social Science Association at Brighton. Entitled *Hygeia: A City of Health* his lecture was a description of an ideal city; the blueprint for a sanitary utopia, an imaginary city with the lowest possible mortality rate. In the years that followed, architects and planners took up many of the ideas in it as they tried to improve living conditions in the overcrowded, polluted towns that were springing up all over Britain, Europe and North America. Ward Richardson designed his solar city for a population of 100,000, living in 20,00 houses, built on 4,000 acres. There were to be an average of 25 people per acre and no house was to be more than four stories in height. No overshadowing from tall buildings was allowed as the city was planned to benefit from the maximum of sunlight. Unfortunately, Dr. Ward Richardson aligned the streets of Hygeia to the points of the compass and may have encouraged later planners to do the same:

*The streets from north to south which cross the main
thoroughfares at right angles, and the minor streets which run
parallel, are all wide, and, owing to the lowness of the houses,
are thoroughly ventilated, and in the day are filled with
sunlight.*

Every house in Hygeia had a garden and its public buildings were
surrounded by lawns, which added to the healthiness of the city. There
were no cellars or basements as all rooms were above ground. Each
house in Hygeia was built on brick arches to ensure good ventilation and
drainage. External brickwork was glazed to prevent the walls becoming
saturated during wet weather. Other unorthodox aspects of the design
included the roofs, the chimneys and the kitchens. For instance, the
chimneys were arranged so that the smoke generated in the fireplaces
passed through a gas furnace before being released into the
environment. Any unburned carbon was consumed and the amount of
air pollution was minimised. The roofs of the houses in Hygeia were flat
and allowed each household to have a roof garden. Kitchens were on the
upper floor of the house rather than the ground floor as in a conventional
dwelling. One advantage of this arrangement was that each kitchen was
'lighted to perfection' so any dust or dirt would be readily detected. In
addition, the smells associated with cooking would not pass through the
house. Hot water from the kitchen boiler would feed the lower rooms.
The bedrooms and bathrooms would be supplied with hot and cold
water and the plumbing of the houses was so arranged to keep out sewer
gases, which Victorian sanatarians greatly feared. The interior of each
house was designed to minimise the risk of disease. Glazed, coloured wall
bricks were specified in place of wallpaper, which Ward Richardson
considered to be unsanitary, and all floors were tiled or of polished wood,
rather than carpeted. The bedrooms were to be large, well-lit, well-
ventilated rooms, which would be kept free of all unnecessary furniture:

*Considering that a third part of the life of man is, or should
be, spent in sleep, great care is taken with the bed-rooms, so
that they should be thoroughly lighted, roomy, and
ventilated... Old clothes, old shoes, and other offensive articles
of the same order, are never permitted to have residence there.*

The inhabitants of Hygeia travelled on an underground railway system
rather than streetcars with their noise and nuisance. This meant there
would be no difficulty in cleaning the spacious wide streets, which were
washed daily. Refuse from the streets was carried away underground with

the city's sewage. The city included industrial units where workers could hire space to carry out their trade. The aim was to prevent people working at home, which Ward Richardson thought was unhealthy. There was a hospital for every 5,000 inhabitants designed with the most up-to-date facilities. These included outpatient and paediatric departments. Ward Richardson considered that several small, temporary hospital buildings would serve the population of Hygeia far better than one large, permanent institution:

> The old idea of warehousing diseases on the largest possible scale, and of making it the boast of an institution that it contains so many hundred beds, is abandoned here.

Each patient was isolated in a separate ward, built of glass and iron, twelve feet high, fourteen feet long and ten feet wide. If at any time a ward needed to be disinfected it could be removed, taken apart and replaced. One end opened onto a corridor, and the other a verandah from which patients could be wheeled out into the hospital garden. The wards were heated by a warm-air mechanical ventilation system powered by a steam engine. As with hospitals, everything in Hygeia associated with health was to be strictly supervised: from the provision of water to the burial of the dead. In this way mortality would be reduced. Dr. Ward Richardson predicted an average mortality of five per thousand per year once the inhabitants of his city had become established. This forecast was made when the annual figure was twenty-two per thousand, and would have been higher in the industrial cities. Ward Richardson predicted that many of the childhood diseases such as croup, diarrhoea and dysentery would be almost unknown. Similarly typhus, typhoid fever and cholera would rarely manifest, while smallpox would be kept under control. Puerperal fever and hospital fever would disappear altogether. Rheumatic fever induced by damp housing would not occur. Above all the number of lives taken by tuberculosis would decrease:

> That large class of deaths from pulmonary consumption, induced in less favoured cities by exposure to impure air and badly ventilated rooms, would, I believe, be reduced so as to bring down the mortality of this signally fatal malady one third at least.

Ward Richardson's Hygeia was unique in being conceived as a city built with the health of its inhabitants as the first consideration. While it may not have been oriented as well as it could have been, Hygeia was the first Utopian city to be planned for the sun for the purposes of hygiene and sanitation. It was conceived two years before Downes and Blunt discovered sunlight's bactericidal effects. Ward Richardson's views on hygiene and healthy buildings differ from those of Florence Nightingale and her supporters in several respects. In particular, the method he proposed for heating his imaginary hospitals, and the size and design of the wards. Nevertheless Dr. Ward Richardson, like Miss Nightingale, recognised that dwellings that were not sunlit were not healthy and he also understood the need to lay out city streets for the sun. Besides his work as a sanitarian, Ward Richardson made significant professional contributions to the disciplines of physiology, pharmacology, pathology, epidemiology, and dental hygiene. He was elected a Fellow of the Royal Society in 1867 and awarded a knighthood in 1893. He devised the motto *'National Health is National Wealth'* that became the rallying cry of the sanitarian movement, and he also invented the metal dustbin.

The Garden City

Following the publication of *Hygeia: A City of Health,* sunlight became prominent in some of the more enlightened English housing projects. In 1879 the Cadbury family moved their cocoa and chocolate factory from the centre of Birmingham to a site five miles to the southwest. The Bournville Village development, which was to become a landmark in urban planning, began in 1895. For its founder, George Cadbury (1839–1922), the level of infection and the number of deaths from tuberculosis in Birmingham was of great concern. More than 10,000 people in the city suffered from the disease and at least 1200 died of it each year. George Cadbury devised Bournville Village with the following objective:

> To make it easy for working men to own houses with large
> gardens secure from the danger of being spoilt either by by the
> building of factories or by interference with the enjoyment of
> sun, light, and air.

In 1888 William Hesketh Lever (1851–1925), later Lord Leverhulme, had begun the construction of his Port Sunlight development with similar objectives to the Cadburys. Leverhulme took a keen interest in architectural matters and social welfare, and shared the same belief in good planning and the benefits of sunlight and fresh air. The principles he developed at Port Sunlight and those of Bournville Village were brought together in the writings of Sir Ebenezer Howard (1850–1928). He put forward the idea of a Garden City in his book *To-Morrow:*

A Peaceful Path to Social Reform of 1898 which was reissued in 1902 as *Garden Cities of Tomorrow.* In writing this Utopian work Howard was motivated by what he saw as the need to try and stop the influx of people from the countryside into already overcrowded, insanitary industrial cities. The Garden City would have its own industry; providing local employment and the promise of a better life for those who moved there. Based on a radial plan reminiscent of Campanella's *City of the Sun,* Howard's Garden City would be circumscribed with an uninhabited green belt, allowing everyone access to open green space. Rings of farms would be created on the outskirts to provide all the food that the residents required, while industry was isolated. Each Garden City was to be totally self-sufficient and would meet all of the needs of its population. The land in these new towns would be communally owned, and subject to collective decisions about its use. The aim was to halt urban sprawl and prevent speculative property developers from building sub-standard housing. Decades later, Howard's thinking informed planners of 'new towns' across the globe, but politically and economically the Garden City never attained his cooperative ideal, nor that of self-sufficiency.

The provision of sunlit dwellings was a guiding principle of the Garden City movement. But streets were not planned for the sun as dogmatically as the solar cities of Greece, or those of Hygeia had been. Instead of being built in rows, the cottages of Bournville and Port Sunlight stand in crescents or squares. Solar access was not as high on the agenda as it had been for Dr. Ward Richardson. It was not, until the inter-war years, that Bournville Village Trust began building solar houses with large south facing windows to admit sunlight for health. At the time, these 'Sunshine Homes', as they were nicknamed by residents, were considered innovative. So, although sunlight was valued from the outset, other objectives were of equal if not more importance. These included keeping industrial and residential areas separate, creating parks and open spaces, replacing closed courts with open streets, and making sure that each house had a garden. Undoubtedly Bournville and Port Sunlight were far healthier places to live than almost anywhere else in industrial Britain at the time. There is good evidence that this was because the residents got more of the sun on them. When the ill-fated Medical Research Committee of 1918 tried to find the cause of rickets there were no national statistics available for analysis. So they visited families in Bournville Village and Port Sunlight and compared their experiences of the disease with those of families living in Glasgow's notoriously dark tenements. The investigators reasoned that if bad housing and lack of fresh air and exercise were factors in the cause of rickets, they could expect to see less of it under better conditions. They found only one case of rickets in Port Sunlight and two at Bournville. By contrast, in Glasgow it was only with the greatest difficulty and after many months that they found enough families free of the disease for their research. There were, however, any number of children with rickets available for examination. The Medical Research Committee may have overlooked sunlight during this lengthy investigation, but at least they provided scientific evidence that planning for the sun prevented disease. The solar city had proven its worth.

Chapter 7
Temples to the Sun

As the sun rose on the architectural world of the 20th century it did so at a time of unprecedented change. Old ways of building were giving way to new. What had traditionally been a craft was turning into an industrial process. New methods of construction, new building materials and standardized, mass-produced components gave designers unprecedented scope for innovation. They could build houses, factories and offices that were radically different from anything that had gone before. With steel and reinforced concrete beams at their disposal they were free to erect large framed structures and span wide spaces. As walls were no longer structural, or load-bearing, they functioned merely as 'curtains'. Windows could be put in them as continuous openings rather than small apertures. Flat roofs began to replace the conventional pitched roof and balconies could be built much more easily. Architects started to enclose large areas in glass and to link interior and exterior spaces visually. These innovations coincided with the rise of the sanatorium movement and a need for highly-glazed, well-ventilated institutions with balconies and terraces where tuberculous patients could receive treatment for their condition.

Even though in retreat, tuberculosis or the 'white plague' as it was known, was still killing more people than all other diseases put together. Much of this death and misery had its origins in the overcrowded dismal housing of industrial towns. Some social reformers saw the Garden City as the solution to society's ills. Others rejected the gabled cottage style of Bournville and Port Sunlight in favour of a more functional approach. Large-scale mechanized construction was the answer; not bricks and mortar. A new style of architecture emerged which embraced the latest technological advances and drew its inspiration from the sunlit dust-free ward of the sanatorium. Many of its leading proponents were involved in sanatorium design. But to them and their followers, Modernism promised much more than the eradication of tuberculosis. It was the pathway to an egalitarian society, to a sunlit socialist Utopia fit for the machine age. The author of the blueprint for this ambitious programme of social reform was the French architect Tony Garnier (1869–1948). Garnier had a high regard for the town planning of Classical Greece and for the hygiene of the tuberculosis ward. He combined the two in a pioneering Utopian work, the *Cité Industrielle,* which was conceived as a solar City of Health just as Ward Richardson's Hygeia had been.

The Cité Industrielle

The Cité project began in 1901 when Garnier was studying in Rome. Detailed plans and perspective drawings were exhibited in 1904 and he continued to work on them until its publication in 1917. Garnier was City Architect of Lyon from 1905 to1919, in which capacity he carried out several projects that owed a great deal to the ideas drafted in his Industrial City.

Fig. 10. The Houses of Tony Garnier's Industrial City

The Cité is composed of a grid of parallel and perpendicular streets aligned with the cardinal points of the compass. Garnier specified that its houses and public buildings were to receive direct sunlight for sanitation. All the dwellings were planned with equal solar access and houses were spaced to prevent shading of adjacent buildings during the winter months. It would be an exaggeration to say that the Cité was conceived as a giant sanatorium, but the way in which the buildings were designed owes a great deal to sanatorium architecture. Garnier also provided the inhabitants of his Utopia with a medical building specifically for sunlight therapy.

Fig. 11. The Heliotherapy Clinic of Garnier's Industrial City

Tony Garnier envisaged that his solar metropolis would be situated in the south-east of France, and would accommodate 35,000 people. Almost all the elements of an actual city were included: factories, administration buildings, social and recreational facilities, and workers' housing. Industrial and residential areas were located in discrete zones with room to expand and develop, and all of the elements were separated by green belts. By zoning the various functions of the Cité and placing so much emphasis on industry, communication and transportation, Garnier expressed ideas that were to preoccupy town planners for years to come. He was also one of the first architects of the 20th century to build in concrete without trying to disguise the fact. He specified reinforced concrete construction throughout his imaginary city. The houses are detached or semi-detached with one or two storeys, and are arranged along a series of long plots facing due south. Like the houses in Ward Richardson's Hygeia they have flat roofs; but what makes them revolutionary is their cubic shape and the fact that they are almost completely depersonalized and make no concessions whatever to previous styles. Tony Garnier summarised the architectural features which were to characterise his residential and public buildings in terms that would have been familiar to the designer of a sanatorium:

1. In residences each bedroom ought to have at least one window, large enough to illuminate the whole room and allow the direct rays of the sun to enter.

2. Courts and light wells, or enclosed spaces used for illumination and ventilation, are prohibited. All spaces, however small, should be lighted and ventilated from the exterior.

3. On the interior of the residences the walls, floors etc. are to be of smooth materials, with rounded corners.

Garnier's solar Utopia was entirely functional, puritanical even, and its cubist housing sympathetic to developments in avant-guarde art. So it must have had an instant appeal for Le Corbusier (1887–1965) who was the first well-known architect to discuss the Industrial City project on its publication. He even referred to it in his own manifesto *Vers une Architecture* in 1923.

Le Corbusier and the Sun

Born Charles-Edouard Jeanneret, at La Chaux-de-Fonds in Switzerland, Le Corbusier was to dominate the architectural world from the 1920s onwards, while his impact on the popular culture of the 20th century ranks with that of Freud, Einstein, and Picasso. Sometimes referred to as the greatest sun-worshipper since Akhenaten, he was a cubist painter, sculptor, theorist, visionary, self-publicist and sunbather. Le Corbusier was a founding member of the *Congres Internationaux d'Architecture Moderne* (CIAM) through which he campaigned for an internationally unified style for modern architecture. Le Corbusier saw architecture and town planning as one. The buildings he designed were components of his own imaginary Utopian cities. Projects such as his *Ville Radieuse* of 1933 feature large apartment blocks standing in open parkland traversed by obsessively straight highways, in the Roman manner. Many of his ideas came to be adopted uncritically by planners of social housing in the post-War municipalities of Europe, North America, and elsewhere. In many respects his vision of the future owes something to Ward Richardson's Hygeia. Every building was to be raised from the ground on supports to provide access for sunlight and fresh air. Also, like the houses in Hygeia they were to have roof gardens. There would be separate zones for workplaces and all the roads would meet at right-angle intersections. But Le Corbusier's approach was markedly different in one respect. Where Dr. Ward Richardson had favoured an underground transport system, Le Corbusier put mass car ownership at the heart of his Utopian vision. He wrote lyrically about the automobile and proposed it as a model for the new architecture. His innovative plans called for super highways to cut across urban centres, improving traffic flow by keeping motor vehicles separate from pedestrians.

Although dedicated to the automobile, Le Corbusier's architecture is also about the sun. He believed it conferred physical and moral regeneration on those who exposed themselves to its rays. He was a keen sunbather, and it is tempting to speculate that he profited from a visit to the sunlight therapy clinics of Dr. Auguste Rollier. There is no documentary evidence that Le Corbusier saw the terraces at Rollier's clinics at Leysin or that he copied them. But as both men shared a common nationality, and were leaders in their respective fields, their paths may have crossed at some point. Le Corbusier published his first propagandist text *Vers une Architecture* in 1923 and Rollier published *L'Héliotherapie,* his best-selling book on sunlight therapy, in the same year. Again, Le Corbusier published the CIAM's manifesto on town planning *The Athens Charter* in 1943, the year before Rollier published his book *Quarante Ans d'Héliotherapie.* How much of Le Corbusier's work derives from Rollier is uncertain, but throughout his extensive writings Le Corbusier shared a similar preoccupation with sunlight and the dangers of tuberculosis. This is clear from the book he wrote in the 1950s on one of his most important buildings; 'L'Unité d'Habitation' or Marseille Block:

> *Doling out cosmic energy, the sun's effects are both physical and moral, and they have been too much neglected in recent times. The results of that neglect can be seen in cemetery and sanatorium.*

The Villa Savoye

The architectural language that Le Corbusier developed from the 1920s onwards reflects such concerns. They find their clearest expression in the Villa Savoye, in Poissy, some 20 miles north-west of Paris. Here, in 1929, his famous 'Five Points of a New Architecture' were crystallized, or made concrete. They were:

- a free-flowing, open-plan interior;
- columns, or 'pilotis', which raise the house above the ground and free the space beneath it;
- a flat roof with roof garden and solarium;
- free façades – because outer walls are no longer load bearing;
- and long horizontal windows.

The living quarters on the first floor of the Villa are surrounded by a ribbon window and face into a sun terrace. This is completely enclosed by the walls of the house and incorporates a ramp that goes up to the top floor. A *promenade architecturale* through the Villa Savoye involves

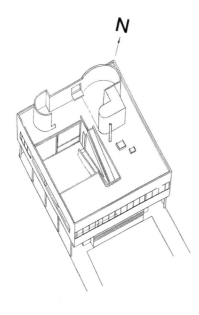

N
/

Fig. 12. The Villa Savoye

climbing a sequence of such ramps and culminates at a sunbathing enclosure on the roof, which is sheltered by a screen of straight and curved walls. That the Villa Savoye is a temple to sunbathing is beyond question; but it should also be recognised as one of the first shrines to the automobile. Le Corbusier designed the house for a car, and not just any car. The Villa hovers above a U-shaped driveway, which matches exactly the turning circle of a chauffeur-driven 1929 Voisin limousine. To get to the front door, the chauffeur had to drive the car under the building, let Monsieur and Madame Savoye alight, and then continue around the curve, either pulling into the garage or out and back to Paris. The automobile was as much at the heart of the design as was the sun. So much so that as well as the Villa Savoye's references to the sunlight therapy clinic, we see in it the green shoots of the drive-in fast food outlet and even, with its internal ramps and reinforced concrete pillars, the multi-storey car park. But again, putting these innovations aside, the Villa Savoye also has much in common with Dr. Rollier's clinic Le Chalet with its open-plan interior, large widows and solarium. Le Corbusier positioned the Villa Savoye on the diagonal, rather than four-square, but not for health reasons. He did so because the site afforded excellent views to the north-west.

L'Unité d'Habitation

Le Corbusier's later work, his L'Unité d'Habitation or Marseille Block, which was built between 1946 and 1952, also incorporates many of the features of a heliotherapy clinic. This monolithic apartment block for 1,600 people was the realisation of the mass housing schemes that had exercised Le Corbusier since the 1920s. He designed L'Unité to alleviate a severe post-war housing shortage in France. Structurally the building consists of a simple reinforced concrete framework, into which are slotted pre-cast apartments, like *'bottles into a wine rack'* as he put it. Twenty-three different types of apartments could be inserted into the structure, providing accommodation for single people or families of ten, and nearly all with double-height living rooms and a frontage on both sides of the building. L'Unité d'Habitation has its own shops, clubs and meeting rooms, all connected by raised 'streets'. There is also a hotel and recreational facilities. Le Corbusier used concrete pilotis to lift L'Unité off the ground rather than the brick arches Dr. Ward Richardson proposed in Hygeia, but the idea was the same.

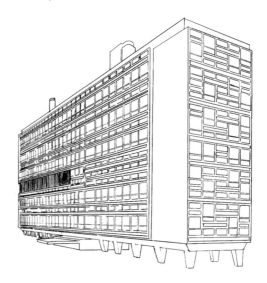

Fig. 13. L'Unité d'Habitation

This milestone of modern architecture is arranged for sunlight. Balconies on both the east and west façades serve as sun-screens or 'brise-soleil' that shade the apartments in the summer months. They are also what Le Corbusier called an 'open-air extension' of each living room. In addition, L'Unité d'Habitation has a terraced roof that provides amenities for the residents, including a gymnasium and a solarium.

As with the Villa Savoye, the prototype for L'Unité d'Habitation may have been built at Leysin, in Switzerland some years earlier under the direction of Dr. Auguste Rollier. The likely candidate, called 'Les Frênes', was the first large purpose-built sunlight therapy clinic to be constructed in Europe. Built in 1911, it consisted of a central, south-facing block and two large wings.

The left wing of the building faced southeast and its upper floors had large uncovered terraces, which could be used for sun treatment year-round. It was in this part of the building that the early morning treatment of the summer months, so favoured by Rollier, took place. As these terraces offered little protection from the wind and summer sunshine, they were used by patients who were well-used to sun treatment, or who were not seriously afflicted by tuberculosis. This wing of the clinic also contained consulting rooms, radiographic departments, rooms for orthopaedics and phototherapy, a bacteriological laboratory, kitchens and offices. On the first floor there was a large hall where patients could

Fig. 14. Les Frênes

be brought to attend films and other forms of entertainment. The central section of the building contained accommodation for non-patient guests and a reception area.

The right wing of 'Les Frênes' faced west of south and patients occupied four of its five floors. There were eight bedrooms on each of the three upper floors and these were reserved for adults. Each room had a private, covered balcony. Partitions between each balcony could be removed so, as with the first floor which was reserved for children, a large recreation or teaching space could be made. The sunlight these bedrooms received was limited because of their orientation. However, they were more sheltered than the terraces on the left wing of 'Les Frênes' and better suited to winter treatment. To compensate for the lack of sun in these covered balconies during the summer months, bedridden patients could be brought up by lift to a solarium that covered the whole roof of the clinic.

The solarium included a covered gallery to provide shelter from the sun, and an arrangement of curtains to give a degree of privacy. The solarium was also used as a play area and by patients who were making their first attempts at walking and who needed absolutely flat ground. In Dr. Rollier's clinic, Les Frênes, we see, for the first time, a vertical self-contained solar community of the kind that Le Corbusier imagined would supersede the conventional city street. However, there is a fundamental difference between Les Frênes and L'Unité d'Habitation in that the former faces south whereas Le Corbusier ran the long axis of L'Unité north-south. In doing so he chose the worst possible orientation for health because this arrangement severely limits the amount of sun the residents get into their apartments in the winter.

Dr. Lovell builds his Health House

The extent to which the greatest sunlight therapist of the 20th century inspired its greatest architect is unclear. But there are some striking similarities between the clinics Dr. Rollier built for his patients and the seminal icons of Modernism created by Le Corbusier. In the United States, evidence that sunbathing for medicinal purposes was the driving force behind Modernism is beyond doubt, at least in California.

The man responsible for the rise of modern architecture on the West Coast was Dr. Philip Lovell, an influential naturopath. Lovell wrote a weekly feature 'The Care of the Body' for the *Los Angeles Times* in which there was much discussion of the benefits of sun and of exercising outdoors, as well as healthy diet. Dr. Lovell promoted natural methods of healing and preventive care, which included a vegetarian diet, massage, water cures, open-air sleeping and nude sunbathing. Lovell wanted a house that encapsulated all that he espoused, and posed a question that still resonates today. He wanted to know how to design a home that would strengthen the health and well-being of its inhabitants. Lovell commissioned the emigré Austrian architect Richard Neutra (1892-1970) to come up with the answer, which he did in 1929. Dr. Lovell's Health House in the Hollywood Hills established Neutra's reputation, bringing him to the forefront of the Modern Movement. His innovative design was a feat of engineering, as it was the first completely steel-framed house in the United States and incorporated some of the most up-to-date manufacturing techniques and mass-produced components.

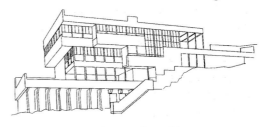

Fig. 15. The Lovell Health House

Built into a steeply sloping site facing west of south, the Health House descends from a street-level floor which has the bedrooms and a study. The living room, kitchen, bathrooms and servant's quarters are on the next level down. Below it, the service level is partially excavated into the hillside. Richard Neutra supported Dr. Lovell's pursuit of the open-air life by providing him with exercise yards, a swimming pool and sports court, and balconies for sleeping outdoors and for nude sunbathing. The balconies are unusual for their time in that they are suspended by steel cables from the roof frame rather than cantilevered out from the building. The Health House is extensively glazed with ceiling-high casement windows giving panoramic views over the city of Los Angeles.

Terraced landscaping provides a connection with nature to promote physical and mental well-being. Richard Neutra designed most of the furniture for the house's interiors too, including tubular steel and bent wood chairs and tables. One of the principles of Modernism was that furniture had to be simple, lightweight and hygienic to prevent dust and bacteria gathering on or beneath it. This idea came from the tuberculosis sanatorium where cleanliness was all important, and before that Ward Richardson's Hygeia. Heavy chairs and tables were an obstacle to hygiene. The Health House was America's first real taste of what was to be come known as the International Style. It is as much a temple to the sun as Le Corbusier's Villa Savoye. Dr. Lovell's Health House appears in several Hollywood movies, including *L.A. Confidential.*

Dr. Lovell's Beach House

The Health House was by no means Dr. Lovell's only venue for nude sunbathing. He had already commissioned another of California's great modern masterpieces – a weekend house at Newport Beach. Built between 1923 and 1926 the Lovell Beach House was the work of the Austrian emigré architect Rudolf Schindler (1887–1953), a former colleague of Richard Neutra's.

Schindler's brief was to exploit the views of the sea and protect Dr. and Mrs. Lovell's privacy from the public beach. Schindler's solution was to raise the house off the ground, which also freed up the space beneath it to form a sheltered outdoor living space complete with its own open fireplace. Rather than employing stilts or pilotis to do this, the architect made a structural skeleton using five parallel, free-standing concrete frames, shaped like square figure-of-eights; these support a two-storey living room which has an interior balcony. This balcony leads to dressing rooms and then to an open sleeping porch that runs along the north façade of the house. This has since been covered over and is no longer open to the elements. Schindler designed the Beach House so that it is penetrated by light on three sides, to the north, south and west. The second floor has uninterrupted views over the

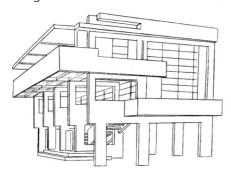

Fig. 16. The Lovell Beach House

ocean. Dr. Lovell sunbathed in private on the roof terrace. One imagines it would have been rather bracing up there because it lacks the permanent screening which Le Corbusier so thoughtfully provided at the Villa Savoye.

The Tugendhat House of Mies van der Rohe

The Villa Tugendhat at Brno, Czechoslovakia was the last major house that Ludwig Mies van der Rohe (1886–1969) designed in Europe before he emigrated to the USA to become the doyen of the steel and glass tower. The house was built between 1928 and 1930, is said to be for Mies van der Rohe what the Villa Savoye represents for Le Corbusier. In some respects the Tugendhat House has more in common with Richard Neutra's Health House in that it sits on a sloping site and backs on to a road, while Le Corbusier was free to orient his Villa as he wished and to lift it above the ground.

The main features are the same though: a vast open-plan living room; extensive glazing; and a terrace on the roof for sunbathing. There are two further suntraps: a south-east facing terrace on the upper floor and a south-west facing terrace on the lower floor, both of which are partly sheltered by the building and so offer more shelter than the roof. The Tugendhat House has most of its glazing on the south and east façades, with the hall and a bathroom facing north. The wall-to-ceiling glazing allows the interior to interact with the exterior in the approved Modernist style.

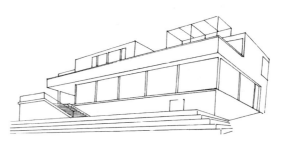

Fig. 17. The Tugendhat House

With no permanent overhangs or roof eaves to keep off the summer sun, Mies van der Rohe had to put adjustable awnings over the south-facing windows to prevent overheating. He also included a notable innovation that linked the interior and outside very effectively. At the touch of a button two large sections of glass slide downwards, disappearing into the basement, converting the living room into an open verandah, or loggia, overlooking the garden.

E. Maxwell Fry's Sun House

The Sun House is the work of one of the few English architects to convert to Modernism and do so with distinction. E. Maxwell Fry (1899–1987) enjoyed the advantage of having worked alongside two of the high priests of the Modern Movement. Between 1934 to 1936 he was in partnership with former Bauhaus director Walter Gropius (1883–1969), after which Gropius moved to the United States to become Professor of Architecture at Harvard University. During their time together, Fry and Gropius designed a school for tuberculous children at Papworth, in Cambridge.

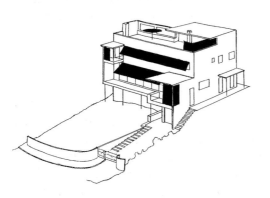

Fig. 18. The Sun House

Then, from 1950 to 1955, Fry collaborated with Le Corbusier on Chandigarh, the new capital of the Punjab in India. Maxwell Fry recognised the hygienic properties of sunlight and of cross-ventilation and no doubt his appreciation of them was heightened by his work on the Papworth project. He particularly valued balconies, which he considered to be a vital release from indoor conditions and an extension to the open air. He brought some of these elements together in his Sun House on a south-facing, sloping site in Hampstead, London. Fry's client required him to make the most of the panoramic views the site offered over the city and to devise a maintenance-free heating system. Unusually for the time Fry specified an automatic gas-fired boiler which supplied hot water to heat elements in the concrete floors. The floors, in turn, acted as storage radiators. The generous glazing on the south façade provided solar gains as well as views. As he wrote in his book *Fine Building* of 1944:

> *Sunlight, not necessarily sunshine, is a form of heating that costs nothing. If dwellings are planned so that the living quarters face the sun, which in England travels across the sky from east to west in a high curve in the summer and a low one in the winter, sunlight entering through generous-sized windows will heat throughout most days of the year, and the large windows will, on balance let in more heat than they let out.*

The Sun House of 1935 is an early example of an English architect designing for energy conservation, and sunbathing. Much use was made of balconies, even to the provision of one from the main bedroom, and of blinds to cut down the ingress of the summer sun. A spacious main staircase gives access to the roof terrace that originally had a permanent windbreak, like the screen at the Villa Savoye. Adjustable curtains were hung from it to further reduce air movement as required. The sheltered suntraps Fry created on the roof terrace were subsequently enclosed and used as storage space, and over the years much of the house's original glazing was replaced. The balcony to the master bedroom was also enclosed and the mechanism for the awnings around the balconies removed. Nevertheless, the Sun House remains an enduring symbol of solar design for both health and energy efficiency, and is aptly named.

Alvar Aalto's Paimio Sanatorium

Finally we come to what is widely regarded as one of the greatest buildings of the last century. Alvar Aalto's tuberculosis sanatorium, now a general hospital, is situated deep in forests about 50 miles west of Helsinki, in Finland. It is built in reinforced concrete and brick and painted white, the colour of hygiene and of the International Style. Throughout the Paimio project, which lasted from 1929 to 1933, Aalto worked closely with the sanatorium's doctors to secure the most therapeutic environment for patients, placing a premium on sunlit spaces. The building is dedicated to sunlight therapy, but not in the same way as the others described above. The people who came to Pamio did so with tuberculosis of the lungs for which direct sun exposure was contraindicated. They were not put out in the sun to tan like patients at a heliotherapy clinic. As they lay in their beds they could enjoy the benefits of fresh air, views of the surrounding countryside, and see the sun but not bathe in it.

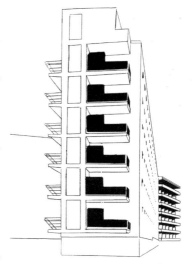

In plan the sanatorium consists of a series of wings that extend from a central spine. The longest and most imposing of these is the seven storey ward block for

Fig. 19. The Paimio Sanatorium

290 patients. This faces south-southeast and was designed so that in the winter the patients would get the full morning sun on their beds.

External shutters enabled hospital staff to regulate the precise amount of sunlight admitted. At the eastern end of the ward block, with its façade facing due south, is the solarium. Cantilevered balconies stacked one above another provide each floor with a place for open-air treatment. There is also a roof terrace, part covered by a canopy, where beds could be wheeled out on warm days. The narrow profile Aalto used for the sanatorium allowed the sun to penetrate deep into the wards and other spaces. It is the care with which he oriented the wards for morning sunlight that is particularly noteworthy. Aalto designed the furniture for the sanatorium, including an all-weather tubular steel framed reclining chair, or *chaise longue*, for patients resting on the sun terraces. He was not alone in this as Le Corbusier and Mies van der Rohe and other architects produced recliners and chairs. These were soon to become modern classics no less than their buildings.

A Question of Orientation

All the buildings described above have solaria and they are arranged to admit sunlight. The Paimio sanatorium is oriented specifically for light therapy. With the Villa Tugendhat, the Sun House, and Dr. Lovell's Health and Beach Houses, the exigences of the site largely determined the orientation. By contrast, Le Corbusier had a free hand. He positioned the Villa Savoye to make the most of the view rather than the sun. This is in itself therapeutic. Studies show that access to views of vegetation, clouds and sky is important for our well-being. Whether a view is as potentially therapeutic as sunlight is doubtful. A view will not kill bacteria nor will it impact on conditions indoors as the sun does. The Villa Savoye is notoriously difficult to keep warm in the winter, something that Le Corbusier might have avoided had he made more of the southerly aspect. Overall, the building engages in rather less of a dialogue with the sun than it might have. Similarly, most of the apartments in his L'Unité D'Habitation face due east and west. Le Corbusier chose this orientation in some of his other projects but it has little to recommend it, as we shall see in the following chapter.

Chapter 8
Making the Most of Light

When the masters of 20th century architecture designed for the sun, the results were mixed. Some were far better at it than others. To understand what this meant for the people inside their buildings, let's return to one of the earliest examples of solar design for health; the Nightingale or pavilion ward. These became so popular throughout Europe, and then North America, that for about 40 years planning hospitals became standardised, or set in stone. Pavilion wards were built with the long axis running north and south. The windows on each side faced east and west between beds placed at right-angles to the external window walls. One major problem with this arrangement is that a building that is placed with its axis north and south like this receives the least sunlight in it in winter, when sunlight is most needed. It also gets too much in summer, when it is most difficult to deal with. At least the pavilion ward shown in Figure 20 has a window on the southern end, which means there would be some sun penetration during the winter, but not that much. The east and west sides would be prone to glare because the sun comes in at a low angle during the summer months, making it difficult to control.

Le Corbusier chose to position his Unité d'Habitation with its long axis running from north to south. Predictably, the apartments at the south end of the block are the most sought after because they get sunlight in the winter and little in the summer. Le Corbusier put shading or 'brise soleils' on both sides of the Unité. On the west façade the apartments also had awnings to screen out the sun completely. Blinds, shutters and curtains will keep the sun out, but they can make an already warm space even warmer by absorbing the sun's heat and reradiating it to the interior. And they make ventilation problematic if they cover window openings. They also cut down light levels to the point where electric lighting is needed. Studying or working indoors in the summer with the blinds down, the lights on and little fresh air does take some of the enjoyment out of it.

The light in rooms illuminated by the rays of the eastern and western sun changes markedly on an hourly and daily basis. This makes them unsuitable places in which to read for any length of time, use sharp objects or operate machinery. West-facing rooms are notoriously difficult to work in because they can become unbearably hot in sunny weather unless they have roof overhangs that are as deep as the windows are tall. The master suite of Dr. Lovell's Health House is at the southwest corner of the first floor and has the best view. But it overheats as it has no overhangs to keep out high-angle sun.

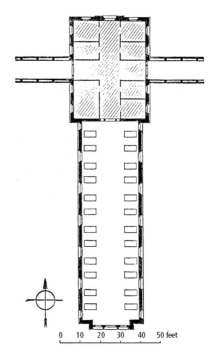

Traditionally, architects reserved a westerly orientation for rooms set aside for rest and relaxation and avoided it for anything else. The Roman custom was to begin work at dawn, finish at midday and bathe after lunch. They built their public baths to face southwest so they could luxuriate in the afternoon sun. It is said that they sometimes used their glazed sun furnaces as 'sweat rooms',

Fig. 20. A Pavilion Ward on a North-South Axis

or solar-heated saunas, and that when the need arose the heliocaminus also doubled as a torture chamber. They simply left their victims to bake. There may be some truth in this because on a sunny day a highly glazed space can get very hot, very rapidly which is why it is so dangerous to leave children unattended in motor vehicles. Apart from the more obvious risks of abduction, or of them getting behind the controls, every year children die from heatstroke in cars and it's not hard to understand why given the temperatures involved. In a study published in the journal *Pediatrics* in 1981 researchers found that if they put a vehicle in direct sunlight when the outdoor temperature was 98.2°F, or 36.8°C, then within 15 minutes the interior was somewhere between 124°F and 153°F, or 51 to 67°C. Most of this heat gain occurred within just 5 minutes of closing the doors. Opening the windows by as much as 8 inches, or 20 cm, had little effect on the temperature rise.

Even in relatively cool conditions on clear, sunny days infants can be at risk for heatstroke. A subsequent study showed that when the surrounding temperature is 72°F, the internal temperature can still reach 117°F, putting unattended children and pets in danger. Anyone left under such conditions in a vehicle, or in a sunlit west-facing room, will experience physical discomfort and physiologic strain, otherwise known as heat stress. Next comes heat exhaustion, a mild to moderate illness associated with dehydration and an increase in core body temperature. The symptoms of heat exhaustion include intense thirst, weakness, anxiety, dizziness, fainting, discomfort, and headache. And finally there's heatstroke, with symptoms such as delirium, convulsions, coma, and death. Although this is most unlikely to happen in a building, it shows just how unpleasant over-glazed and badly oriented spaces can be, especially if they face west. This is why highly glazed buildings consume so much energy. Heating them is not so much of a problem: keeping them cool is. The 'gas-guzzling glass stump' beloved of Modernists and multinational corporations is so-called because of the amount of air conditioning needed to keep the interior habitable in sunny weather.

Orientation for Health

Returning to the pavilion ward for a moment, today the way to orient a long, narrow building such as this would be to place the long axis east-west so one side faces due south and the other due north. With this approach, fixed horizontal overhangs, or roof eaves, can exclude high-angle summer sunlight from the south. Then in the winter, when the sun is lower in the sky, its rays pass beneath the overhangs, and can penetrate and warm the interior. A south-facing orientation is widely recommended as being most suitable for saving energy; and it's the one the Greeks used 2,500 years ago. There are two disadvantages, however, with an east-and-west position. The first is the area of complete shadow on the north side of the building during one-half of the year, and the second is that there is more overshading, or a longer shadow than with any other position. So if a hospital planner wanted to get as many Nightingale wards on a site as possible while keeping them out of shadow, this is the worst arrangement. A greater distance would be needed between the pavilions than with any other orientation. The two intermediate positions, northeast-southwest and northwest-southeast, would be better; there is little to choose between them as far as the sunlight they receive during different seasons is concerned. By placing windows at the southeast or southwest end, as the case may be, the amount of sunlight they admit in winter would be increased. But the big advantage of diagonal siting is that buildings can be placed closer together than in either of the other two positions. And they can be planned so that all of the outside walls are exposed to the sun at some portion of the day throughout the year.

The difference between the northeast-southwest and the northwest-southeast positions is that in the former the broad side of the building gets the sun in the morning, while the latter gets it in the afternoon. From what we know of heliotherapy and SAD, sunlight is more therapeutic earlier in the day than in the afternoon because it is constantly increasing in intensity, while in the afternoon it is constantly decreasing. Also sunlight is more valuable as an energy source in the morning, as it heats the building up when it needs heating, rather than later in the day when it may already be warm. So, for buildings in or near the latitude considered in this book, the long axis should be placed as nearly northeast and southwest as possible, and, further, the southwest end should always have windows. Of course, if someone decides to build a Roman bath and wants some sun in the afternoon, then a northwest-southeast orientation would be the better choice.

More compact buildings need a slightly different approach, although the basic principle is much the same, as William Atkinson explained in his lectures 100 years ago. For health and hygiene a square building should be set on the diagonal, with the living room, or the rooms that are used most often during the day, placed at the southern apex. Clearly, much depends on the site and the amount of sun available; and also the intended use of the space within the building. Where people sit in fixed positions for long periods, direct sunlight can be unwelcome. Where they can move into and out of patches of sunlight, the variety and stimulus it brings is valued and it makes interiors more dramatic and attractive. Vitruvius left us instructions for the orientation of rooms for comfort and energy-saving. He said that winter dining rooms should face in a westerly direction to get the afternoon sun for warmth and light, and bedrooms should get the morning sun. Vitruvius made no mention of kitchens. But if he had he would probably have counselled against westerly orientation because a kitchen facing this way would get very hot in warm weather. Heat from cooking would be augmented by heat from the sun. Rooms that do not benefit from sunlight or are not occupied frequently, such as hallways, utility rooms, and stores, should be placed to the north. However, it is difficult to be too specific, because people have their own preferences where sunlight is concerned. Some like a sunlit bedroom while others do not.

Until the middle years of the last century, natural lighting largely determined the plan of a building and the design of its external envelope; the Nightingale ward being a case in point. But with the advent of low-wattage fluorescent tubes in the 1930s, and air conditioning, reflective glass and cheap energy, the urban landscape began to change. Daylight was no longer a critical design element, as these technological advances made lighting deep-plan buildings a practical proposition. This is reflected in hospital design where, for all its faults, the light, airy pavilion ward came to be replaced by complex structures where even on the sunniest days the windows are shut and fluorescent tubes are ablaze. And so, with the passage of time, the skills needed to light buildings for health were lost.

Solar design did enjoy a revival in the 1970s following a dramatic rise in fuel prices reminiscent of those in ancient Greece and Rome. With much enthusiasm, but often with little knowledge of the subject, architects began building solar homes to try to reduce energy demand. Some worked well but looked decidedly odd, while others performed poorly because they had too much glazing, or misplaced windows, inadequate shading, poor siting or other factors working against them. As sunlight is such a dynamic source of heat and light, harnessing its energy can be challenging. The position and intensity of the sun continuously varies. In cloudy weather its output is unreliable, and from dusk until dawn the sun disappears below the horizon and its energy is beyond use. Matters are not helped by an added complication: using sunlight for one purpose, such as heating, is not always easy to reconcile with using it for lighting, or health.

Unfortunately, rather than acquire the traditional skills and knowledge to bring these elements together, contemporary building design has turned its back on the sun and walked away. Solar architecture is the exception rather than the rule, and few modern architects or builders fully understand the principles and benefits involved. After all, it is much easier to make a building energy-efficient by putting in lots of insulation and sophisticated controls, rather than to let the sun and air in. Yet this ignores the response of human beings to living and working in an artificial environment, and to light deprivation. Designers get away with this because sadly, in marked contrast to the citizens of Imperial Rome, we do not have a right to sunlight. Architects and developers are not under any legal obligation to provide us with it. Some communities in the United States have solar access laws that protect the south side of buildings from overshading. These ensure access to sunlight for solar energy devices. There are any number of cities around the world that have zoning ordinances demanding public access to sunlight in the streets. But none that stipulate sunlight in dwellings. Building illumination codes do not address light and health, nor do they assign compulsory illumination levels. Lighting codes and standards are mainly concerned with visual performance and the elimination of glare. They often list optimal illuminances for different tasks, but do so based on constant, uniform levels of artificial light falling on the working plane, and not on the retina. The illumination levels required for light therapy to be effective are several times higher than those recommended for visual task performance in most buildings.

Toilets or Corridors	100-150 lux
Canteen or Restaurants	200 lux
Classroom or Library	300-500 lux
Workbench	500 lux
General Office	500 lux
Drawing Office	500-750 lux
High-precision tasks	1,500 lux
Bright Light Therapy	2,500-10,000 lux

Table 1. Some typical recommended illuminances.

As far as the law is concerned, windows are there to provide us with ventilation and an escape route in case of fire. The fact that they provide natural light is a bonus. While there are rights to skylight in Britain, access to sunlight is not protected which means that it is acceptable in law to block out someone else's sun.

Skyscrapers and the Sun

A problem that will become increasingly common in Britain and elsewhere in the years ahead is over shading from tall buildings. Skyscrapers are back in favour with politicians, planners and architects, and so there are going to be a lot more of them. High-rise buildings first became fashionable during the 1920s when the architectural elite decided they were the healthiest and most efficient solution to the problem of providing homes in overcrowded city centres. The tower block became the ultimate symbol of their Utopian vision, and a tool with which to break with the past and do away with traditional housing. Leading advocates, such as Le Corbusier and Walter Gropius, argued that high-rise, high-density dwellings would prevent urban sprawl and at the same time 'aerate' the city. Modernists transformed the heliocentric architecture of the tuberculosis sanatorium into the high-rise tower. Slums became vertical, rather than horizontal. Tower blocks proved a failure as social housing for low-income families, especially those with children, and there is no evidence that they prevent suburbs from spreading outwards. High-rise developments do not necessarily achieve greater densities than mid- or low-rise ones and sometimes make less efficient use of the available land. Nor is there any evidence that people living near the top of a tower block enjoy air that is any more wholesome than for people living near the bottom. True, residents may have unrestricted access to sunlight, but they do so at the expense of people nearby in shorter, older buildings. Skyscrapers cast long, unhealthy shadows and, historically, the principal means of protecting access to natural light has been by restricting the height of buildings. No one who understands the importance of light to health would encourage their construction. In recent years there have been concerted efforts to reinvent skyscrapers as examples of so-called 'sustainable' or 'bioclimatic' architecture, and so reduce the damage they inflict on the environment. But tall buildings are about power, status, vanity and aesthetics. The taller they are the longer the shadow they throw. Some people like to look at them, and others like to take in the view from the top. But if right-to-sunlight legislation were to be reintroduced there would be fewer opportunities for such sightseeing, because there would be an immediate moratorium on high-rise construction. Predictably in Boston, Massachusetts a hundred years ago, our old friend William Atkinson took a dim view of tall buildings, and one of his finest achievements was to stop the skyscraper in its tracks. As he wrote in 1905:

> We must not consider these tall buildings separately. We must consider them as if the whole street were built up with them, because that is the condition to which we are rapidly coming in cities in this country. In making building laws and planning streets we should look into the future and not merely regard the present.

In 1904 Atkinson had been a member of a committee at the Boston Society of Architects that helped to draft legislation regulating the height of buildings. The aim was to preserve the right of Bostonians to sunlight

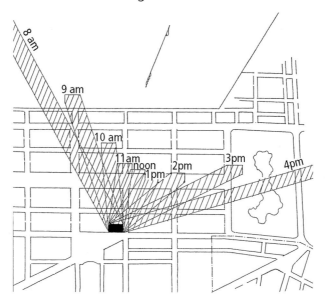

*Fig. 21. William Atkinson's Diagram of the Shadow Cast
by Skyscraper in Winter in Boston, Mass.*

under the law, and to put their health before landowners' and builders' profits. Boston's tradition of sunlit streets, and the new law that guaranteed them, was challenged soon afterwards in a case that went right to the top of the American judicial system, to the Supreme Court in Washington. A property developer named Welch had been keen to take advantage of the latest high-rise technology and make Boston's buildings taller and rents fatter. Mr. Welch and his lawyers challenged the constitutionality of William Atkinson's zoning law, but fortunately the US Supreme Court upheld it in 'Welch v. Board of Appeal of the City of Boston' on May 17, 1909. On this occasion the health of the people really was the highest law. Figure 21 shows one of Atkinson's drawings of a 300 foot tall building in Boston and the shadow it would cast in midwinter. By banning skyscrapers William Atkinson ensured that Boston remained a sunlit city rather than one in shadow. This, in turn, meant there was less vitamin D deficiency, and less disease.

The mediaeval streets of the City of London appear destined to become as dark as they were during the Industrial Revolution, only this time it will be skyscrapers that obscure the sun rather than air pollution. And even where sunlight is still visible, glare and overheating are now of such concern to the design community the sun is being screened from direct view in new buildings, and windows positioned and oriented to keep it out. Unless access to the sun is recognised as a fundamental human right in the near future, which is unlikely, there is little imminent prospect of solar legislation appearing on the statute books.

Electric Light and Health

During the last 30 years scientists have shown that artificial light has a direct influence on the body's immune system and that it can strengthen or compromise our health. Bulbs and fluorescent lamps have been developed that mimic sunlight indoors and are called 'daylight' or 'full-spectrum'. The term full-spectrum refers to a light source that contains the full range of colours of the visible spectrum and in some cases ultraviolet radiation as well. Conventional household light bulbs are deficient in the green-blue area of the light spectrum and almost totally lacking in UV radiation. Ordinary 'cool-white' fluorescent tubes are deficient in the red and blue-violet ends of the spectrum, while having excessive levels of orange and yellow. Full-spectrum lights come in one of four types: incandescent bulbs; halogen lamps; fluorescent tubes; and compact fluorescents. Some of the lamps on sale are more 'full-spectrum' than others: their quality or specification can vary considerably. While none are as strong as the lamps used in phototherapy for SAD, they can offer better indoor clarity than conventional bulbs and some strip-lights, and in doing so may reduce eye strain and fatigue. Also, fine colour judgements can be made more accurately under a full-spectrum fluorescent lamp than under a conventional cool-white one. As we evolved under the solar spectrum it seems reasonable to assume that we are at our best in daylight; and that artificial light should reflect this. After all, the human circadian system is better matched to the spectrum of daylight than that of cool-white fluorescent lamps or incandescent bulbs.

However, the health benefits of using full-spectrum lighting are still a matter of much debate within the scientific community. Some studies suggest they are beneficial while others do not. A literature review published in the journal *Psychological Medicine* in 2001 concluded that evidence for any positive health outcomes is weak. But as with the research on phototherapy for depressive illnesses – which remained inconclusive for years – confounding factors often play their part. In particular, daylight must be always be excluded before any valid comparisons can be made between different artificial light sources. While we wait for this to be resolved it is worth bearing in mind that the output of full-spectrum lamps is fixed. It cannot follow the variation in light spectrum that occurs outdoors with time, and with seasonal changes and with weather conditions. Also some full-spectrum lamps produce less light per unit of electrical energy than cool-white lamps; and while some people prefer them, others do not.

People who live in environments where they have little or no access to solar exposure require vitamin D from a source other than sunlight. They have two choices: supplements or ultraviolet radiation. The perceived wisdom is that taking vitamin D supplements is inherently safer than synthesizing vitamin D in the skin. The use of UV lamps or sunbeds is actively discouraged because of concerns about increased skin cancer risks. We are told that if extra vitamin D is required – and clearly for many people it is – then supplements rather than sunbeds should be used. While there are risks associated with using sunbeds, taking oral vitamin D can be dangerous. There is no direct evidence that sunbeds cause malignant melanoma. Nor are there any reports of vitamin D intoxication after intensive exposure to UV radiation. Also, the absorption of dietary vitamin D via the intestines becomes less efficient as we age. Vitamin D activated by UV radiation bypasses any malabsorption. A study published in the *American Journal of Clinical Nutrition* in 2004 showed that people who use sunbeds regularly have twice the levels of vitamin D in their blood and significantly stronger bones than those who do not. And research shows that one way to overcome vitamin D deficiency in the elderly is to expose them to ultraviolet radiation from a lamp. This is precisely what doctors used to do to children in the days of rickets and tuberculosis. Again, there has never been a proper assessment of the risks and benefits. So no one knows which is the healthier option; sunbeds or supplements.

24-Hour Lighting

Lighting interior spaces for vision can be demanding because individual needs and tastes vary so much depending on the task being undertaken, the ability and age of the person trying to carry it out, and the setting. Lighting for health is even more demanding because the basics have yet to be determined. Exactly how much light is needed to entrain the circadian system depends on its intensity, duration, the spectrum of light and the timing of exposure to it. So far, we know we need to spend time in brightly lit spaces during the day, and then dimly lit spaces in the evening as the body prepares for sleep. We also need darkness at night;

and a gradual increase in light levels around dawn can be helpful. However, more people now work at night than ever before. They may be harming themselves by doing so. Again, research is in its early stages, but there could be a dark side to our increasingly 24-hour culture. Shift-workers are trying to work when their bodies are telling them to sleep, and trying to sleep when the world is awake, which leaves them permanently jet-lagged with their immune systems potentially compromised. The harmful effects of working at night include a higher incidence of cardiovascular disease, of gastrointestinal problems and of psychological disorders. Then there is the greater incidence of breast and colon cancer among women exposed to light at night. So far no definite cause and effect can be made between light, disruption of circadian rhythms, and cancers. But evidence is mounting that there is a link, just as there is between cancers and vitamin D deficiency. And this is happening when advances in lighting technology have made night-time lights brighter than ever before with more blue wavelengths in them. Great for vision but not so good for health. Also, research shows that shortened or disturbed sleep can lead to reduced insulin sensitivity, which in turn may result in an increased risk of metabolic disorders, including obesity. It seems the chances of someone becoming obese depend on the quantity and quality of sleep they get, as well as the amount of exercise they take, their diet and their vitamin D levels. People who work at night and sleep when the sun is out appear to be at particular risk of obesity.

Another of the hazards of shift-work is the incidence of accidents. Some of the world's biggest environmental disasters, such as the one at the Chernobyl nuclear plant in 1986, happened at night. There is a seasonal pattern to accidents too. A study published in *Psychiatry Research*, in 1995, showed that 58 per cent of all medication errors in a hospital in Alaska happened during the first quarter of the year. Such errors were 1.95 times more likely in December than September, and followed a pattern closely associated with the annual cycle of daylight and darkness. One solution to this is to take medical staff and shift-workers to one side and give them some precisely timed light exposure to boost their serotonin levels and suppress their melatonin secretion. Another would be to configure lighting systems to keep them alert at all times, although the duration, intensity and spectrum of the light used to do this would have to be identified first.

Clearly, there are major opportunities for developing lighting technologies that promote safety and health. New methods of making light are coming on the market. Conventional household bulbs are yielding market share to optoelectronic products, such as light-emitting diodes (LEDs) and other technologies. There are now ways of making artificial light dynamic so it will match the way daylight changes in colour and intensity from dawn to dusk. Soon designers will be able to simulate outdoor lighting conditions indoors from the moment the sun rises until it sets. The temptation will then be to exclude natural light altogether and do it all artificially. This has some attractions of which the most obvious, to some at least, is the sun can be kept out. Life then becomes much easier for everyone involved in procurement and design of buildings because it requires a lot less thought and expertise. However, the lighting industry now has to adapt to ever more severe energy and environmental legislation. How such developments will translate into practical lighting applications in the years ahead is far from certain. But it will be far less damaging to the environment and far more therapeutic to let in a modest amount of sunlight than to keep it out altogether.

Chapter 9
The Light Revolution

Throughout history architects and engineers built for the sun. In the ancient world much of this work was undertaken for religious purposes; to facilitate sun worship and mark the sun's movements across the heavens. There was also an appreciation that sunlit buildings could save energy and prevent disease. Unfortunately, the human race has lost sight of this on more than one occasion.

Imagine being in the privileged position of building a house from scratch and of wanting to make the most of the sunlight in and around it. In an urban setting the house would, of necessity, be part of a new or existing development. Ideally, this would itself be planned for the sun. The main thoroughfares would be carefully oriented towards what used to be called the 'winter east' and the 'winter west'. As we have already seen, in temperate regions this means that they would be inclined at about 45° to the meridian. But the precise alignment depends on the latitude of the site. Also the streets would be wide enough to prevent overshading from nearby buildings. The city of Milton Keynes, in Bedfordshire, England is a rare example of modern solar planning along these lines. The orientation of Milton Keynes is almost correct for its latitude and its streets run at right angles to each other. Also, Milton Keynes is home to a number of solar dwellings, although these are designed for energy efficiency and not for health.

There are many excellent publications on solar design for energy thrift, but very little guidance on the solar architecture of health, which is why this book has been written. Again, as mentioned previously, the fundamental difference between the two approaches to solar design is that the outside of a dwelling built for health is arranged for the sun. Another is that the building and the rooms within it are positioned to exploit sunlight's therapeutic qualities. Also, wherever possible dual-aspect fenestration is specified to allow sunlight into living spaces at different times of the day, or year, to entrain the body's diurnal and seasonal rhythms. Natural ventilation is the preferred means of getting fresh air in and stale air out. Where practicable, rooms are cross-ventilated in the manner both of the Nightingale ward and some of the better tuberculosis sanatoriums. And finally an underfloor, or radiant heating system has traditionally been specified in such dwellings to supplement or augment the radiant heat of the sun. To summarize, if we had to put together 'Five Points of Solar Architecture for Health' after Le Corbusier, they would be:

1. Orient the building for sanitation and sunbathing.
2. Position the rooms for sunlight therapy and disinfection.
3. Put windows in more than one wall to let the sun in at different times of the day or year.
4. Ventilate naturally.
5. Underfloor heating.

The Romans were fond of underfloor heating. They passed warm air beneath the floors of their bath complexes and villas. The Roman 'hypocaust' created radiant internal surfaces, which supplemented the heat of the sun. Perhaps they thought it was the healthiest way to heat a building. Research published in the 1920s suggests that underfloor heating is indeed healthier than other methods. At this time the thinking was that the environment within a building should be as close as possible to ideal outdoor conditions, namely: cool breezes around the head; the radiant heat of the sun; and warm ground to stand on. Several leading architects of the period, such as E. Maxwell Fry, included underfloor heating in their designs. Fry, like the Romans, had an eye on health and energy efficiency.

Having identified a few key points of solar design for health, what of an existing dwelling? Unfortunately, it can be difficult to change a building's orientation without knocking it down and starting again. Nevertheless, there is often scope for an improvement of one kind or another. The first requirement is for a sunny, sheltered, private place for sunbathing. George Bernard Shaw's shed would be ideal, but a less elaborate structure would do. The second is somewhere sheltered for morning exercises during the winter months, and the third is provision for drying laundry outside in the sun for as much of the year as possible. This disinfects it and releases moisture from washing into the atmosphere, rather than indoors. One way to meet some of these requirements is to add a conservatory or sun lounge to a property. But these come with a health warning: point them in the wrong direction and in sunny weather they heat up just as the interior of a motor vehicle does. Also, it can be tempting to use a conservatory as living space throughout the year. This means keeping it warm in winter, which is both wasteful of energy and costly. A less expensive alternative is a porch or verandah, which would at least keep the worst of the winter weather off when taking early morning exercise. These were once a standard feature of hospitals and nursing homes in the days when light and air were valued, and vitamin D deficiency was more of a concern than it is today. Elderly people, particularly those who are deficient in vitamin D, are prone to falls and fractures. One way to make a building safer is to get sunlight on paths and driveways to keep them dry and prevent falls on snow and ice in the winter. They are difficult to reorientate once established, but sometimes vegetation and other obstructions can be cleared away to let more sunlight on to them. A patio or terrace can be a useful amenity for sunbathing and exercise, with the added benefit that if positioned beneath glazing it will reflect sunlight into a building.

Window glass can itself be a hindrance to illumination, at least for health. Glass not only filters out the UVB radiation that triggers the synthesis of vitamin D in the skin, but it also absorbs light. A single-glazed window with a pane of clear float glass in it will transmit about 85 per cent of the light incident upon it. Double- or triple-glazing will reduce the light transmitted to the interior to about 70 per cent and 60 per cent respectively. The selective 'low-e' energy efficient double glazing specified in new buildings has a heat loss equivalent to that of triple glazing, and a light transmission factor of about 80 per cent. The tinted glasses used in offices and factories reduce glare and solar heat gain to some extent, but also cut down daylight transmission and distort its spectrum. Reflective windows used in high-rise buildings block as much as 50 per cent of the solar radiation incident upon them. Like tinted glass, they reduce the transmission of the sun's light as well as its heat, and continue to do so in winter when bright light is of most value. By contrast, during the 1930s, there were offices, factories, hospitals and homes with special UV-transmitting glass in the windows. The idea was to get as many of the sun's 'chemical rays' indoors as possible. Manufacturers still produce it but there is less demand for UV-transmitting glass than there was in the heyday of heliotherapy. Another way to gain direct access to the sun's UV radiation is to install windows that slide out of the way, as Mies van der Rohe did at his Tugendhat House.

A Light Audit

One thing to do whenever viewing a property, or a potential site, is to take a compass and use it to help build a mental picture of the sun's movements throughout the year. Another piece of equipment, which can be most useful, is a digital lux meter. Take one of these around a building during the day with all the lights off and see what the readings are. The results can be illuminating even if the building is not. Keep a record of the light levels indoors and the direction from which the light comes. Such an exercise involves making a room-by-room analysis of the home or workplace. A simple diary or audit kept over days and weeks can give a useful insight into the quality, quantity, timing and direction of sunlight coming into a dwelling. Having identified any deficiencies, there may be opportunities to increase the direct, or indirect sunlight being admitted. Given enough resources and a free hand, the obvious path to take would be to reposition, enlarge or put more openings in the building fabric. This is not something to be undertaken without detailed knowledge of the site, the building and the sun's movements throughout the year. Familiarity with some of the finer points of solar design for energy efficiency would be an advantage too.

A less radical approach involves reviewing the use of interior spaces, and making the most of any sunlight that does come in. The idea is to follow the sun: start in one room in the morning or in the spring, and then move to another in the afternoon, or the autumn. But the simplest way to make the most of sunlight is to use interior finishes and colours that reflect it. Having entered a room, sunlight and skylight repeatedly bounce off the ceiling, the walls, the floor and the fixtures and fittings. Each time this happens some of their energy is absorbed and light is lost. Smooth white walls and ceilings reflect about 80 per cent of the light that falls on them, yellow ones about 60 per cent and so on through the colours. One way to reflect more sunlight into a room is to paint soffits, mullions, and window reveals white. This is a traditional strategy for getting light into rooms and is a feature of the Georgian terraced house. A more complex and expensive way is to install a 'lightpipe', a device that gathers sunlight with mirrors or lenses and then channels it down a shaft, or fibre-optic cables to wherever it is needed. Unlike a window, lightpipes can only deliver reflected light and not a direct view of the sun. Nevertheless, they do give some relief from the monotony of electric lighting and can bring natural light to spaces that would otherwise not see any at all. The judicious placement of mirrors can also do a great deal to improve lighting levels in dark spaces. But let us return to the bigger picture. There is much that could be done to render such remedial work unnecessary – not in existing buildings, unfortunately, but in those that will be constructed in the years ahead.

The North Point is Missing

The 20th century's greatest architect, Le Corbusier, advocated solar planning and built for the sun. He was not particularly good at it. Nor were some of the other architects who tried it. But then astronomy is not studied as it once was. Modern designers are not as familiar with the sun's movements as they might be. And orientation is not always uppermost in their thoughts. An indicator of this is that one essential detail is often missing from architectural plans and drawings – the north point of the compass. Anyone who doubts this should go to an architectural library and look up the Villa Savoye. Some authors say it faces south. Others say it faces southeast or northwest, or make no mention of its orientation at all. And Le Corbusier left us little to go on other than the building itself. If someone so widely admired and copied could pay so little attention to the orientation of his works it is not surprising that there are dark spaces where there need not be.

When the likes of Le Corbusier and Mies van der Rohe were establishing their reputations the link between bad housing and disease was more obvious than it is now. Then the great scourge was tuberculosis. In developing countries it still is. But in the industrialised world the ill-effects of sedentary indoor lifestyles are nearer the top of the public health agenda: obesity; heart disease; diabetes; and depression to name a few. And beneath all this runs an undercurrent of vitamin D deficiency. Medicine will not solve these problems. Prevention is required not treatment. Now is the time for a built environment that puts health first. Modernists tried to do this when they confronted tuberculosis at the beginning of the last century. But they passed down an unhappy legacy, especially where urban planning is concerned. Although they were keen to demolish anything they thought was bad, they were unable to produce much that was substantially better. By putting the automobile before the pedestrian and the cyclist they created a new set of problems that will take some time to resolve.

The historic link between urban planning and public health has been broken, and matters are not helped by the fact the building community attaches more importance to environmental concerns than to health, for reasons that are understandable. The world's climate is changing. It has a history of doing so. Some scientists predict that average temperatures will increase by several degrees over the next century and will make parts of the developing world uninhabitable. This impending catastrophe is attributed to rising levels of carbon dioxide in the atmosphere. However, events surrounding the Maunder Minimum suggest that solar activity may play a larger part in climate change than is generally acknowledged. To say so invites ridicule, because to question orthodoxy on such matters is tantamount to religious heresy. Nevertheless, anyone who has watched leading experts and pundits denouncing sunbathing over the last 20 years could be forgiven for being a little sceptical about some of the claims being made. We may be looking at a global disaster of our own making, or we may not. Based on experience, when faced with a moral crusade driven by an alliance of scientists and politicians, it pays to be cautious.

If temperatures do rise significantly they will have an impact on the indoor environment; especially in the summer months when there will be a greater risk of buildings overheating. A warmer climate will, in turn, have a direct influence on the amount of light within buildings. The preferred way to prevent summertime overheating is to limit heat gains from the sun. Unfortunately this may result in even more bright light being designed-out of buildings than it is at the moment, and just as its importance to health is finally being recognised. Arranging the built environment in anticipation of an environmental catastrophe that may or may not happen is one thing, but to do so at the expense of the inhabitants is another matter, and that is what appears to be happening. It is unquestionably a good idea to make the best use of our resources and to eliminate waste and pollution. However, dwellings that perform well in energy and environmental terms are not necessarily the most life enhancing. A balance needs to be struck between the two, as individuals who are in good health and are productive need less energy to sustain them and support their activities than those who are unwell. For example, if sunlight speeds up the recovery of hospital patients and lessens their use of drugs, then it will also reduce the energy consumed when looking after them. Somewhere between 70 and 90 per cent of the costs of running hospitals and other large organisations consist of the salaries of the workforce. The financial returns for employers who provide healthy sunlit spaces could be considerable, as could the energy savings. There is no official method that can be used to quantify the impact of improved patient outcomes, worker productivity, or staff retention on energy consumption. With no established procedures for putting a value on them it becomes difficult to present a hard case for healthy lighting, or healthy anything else.

A Right to Sunlight

The Romans did what they could to prevent disease; and sunlight played its part in this. Among other things they arranged their public baths for the sun. Similarly during the 1930s, when doctors promoted sunbathing as a public health measure, open-air swimming pools often included facilities for taking sun baths. Architects designed for this just as they had in Imperial Rome. Of course, there are risks to sun exposure as there are to swimming or riding a bicycle. So far, no one has put together a public health campaign to try to discourage people from cycling or swimming. They would have to present a convincing case and a large body of scientific evidence before anyone took them seriously. Or would they? Government agencies and medical experts have exhorted us to avoid the sun without first assessing the risks and benefits of doing so. Had they been familiar with the unfortunate story of rickets from 1650 to 1921 they might have been a little less cavalier, or negligent. Health campaigns that promote sun avoidance and are designed to engender a fear of sunbathing almost inevitably add to the prevalence of vitamin D deficiency. This is common across all age groups. There is even a resurgence of rickets among children, half a century after it was thought to have been eliminated. What little time urban populations now spend outdoors should be spent in the sun rather than hiding from it. There is enough evidence of a link between vitamin D deficiency and cancer, cardiovascular disease and the rest, for health campaigns to be put in place that promote sunbathing rather than discourage it. This may happen once definitive proof becomes available, but it could be a long wait. And here is an example of how we differ from the Romans. Where public health was concerned, they relied on experience, observation, common sense and the skills of their engineers, rather than curative medicine. They drained swamps or built well away from them because they knew marshland was unhealthy; a place of fevers and flying insects. Had they waited for scientists to prove that mosquitoes carry malaria before draining marshland the Roman Empire would probably have ended a lot sooner than it did.

Based on the available evidence, inadequate vitamin D levels due, in part, to a fear of sunlight may have caused thousands of people in Europe, the United States and elsewhere to die prematurely, many more than have died from skin cancer. If a campaign to promote sunbathing were introduced to reverse this unfortunate state of affairs it might be fraught with problems. Telling the populace to do something is easy. The hard part is getting them to do it having told them not to for 20 years. A degree of confusion would follow and a few reputations would be tarnished along the way. More importantly, hospitals, nursing homes, and leisure facilities are no longer designed for the sun, so getting out into it can be a problem, particularly for the elderly, the infirm or immobile.

Much is made of the need to make modern buildings sustainable and energy efficient. But they are not sustainable if they are unhealthy, and they are unhealthy if they keep the sun out. Our minds and bodies need light at therapeutic levels for some of the time that we are awake. Such levels are way above those typically found indoors nowadays. Conventional lighting strategies enable us to see well enough to perform visual tasks, but they keep us in biological darkness during the daytime and an unnaturally bright environment at night. Indoors, behind glass, interior lighting gives somewhere between 50 to 500 lux, while outdoors the range is 1000 to 100,000 lux, or more. Electric lights are expensive to run, especially at the intensities needed to entrain the body's circadian system and suppress melatonin secretion. Sunlight is cheaper and less harmful to the environment but, unfortunately, it can be difficult to get the sun indoors. Cities and towns are not laid out for it, skyscrapers block it out and the skills needed to arrange buildings for the sun are in very short supply. No one is under any obligation to build for the sun. The health benefits of solar design are not widely recognised and there are no rights to sunlight.

The Romans had sun-right laws. But we have no real way of knowing whether their solar legislation and solar buildings improved the life expectancy of the Roman citizen. However, their policy of putting public health in the hands of engineer-architects rather than doctors may have yielded large dividends. There is evidence that by insisting on clean water for drinking and bathing they may have improved their chances of seeing old age. A paper published in the journal *Demography* in 2005 shows that introducing water filtration and chlorination in major U.S. cities from the 1900s onwards resulted in the most rapid health improvements in the nation's history. Deaths from water-borne diseases such as typhoid fever and from other infections declined sharply. Clean water was responsible for nearly half the total fall in mortality in major cities in the first 40 years of the 20th century. This included three-quarters of the fall in infant mortality and nearly two-thirds of the fall in child mortality. Although the

Romans lacked the technology with which to chlorinate water, they did not discharge human waste into their aqueducts and so had little need of it. During the 19th century, and into the 20th, as often as not drinking water in cities came from rivers contaminated with raw sewage, which is why filtration and chlorination had such an impact.

Perhaps we should follow the Roman's example and keep the medical profession from the forefront of public health. It might prove to be a more cost-effective approach. Unfortunately we differ from the Romans in that our architects are not as well-versed in medicine as theirs appear to have been. Without a grounding in infection control, physiology and phototherapy it is difficult to see how ours can design hospitals, or indeed any other type of dwelling, to prevent disease. Few now have the ability to gauge the interaction between buildings and occupants; and if architects cannot act as intermediaries who else can? We need designers who know how to work with sunlight to exploit its healing powers to the full. But a more pressing need is for right-to-sunlight legislation and the will to enforce it. Without laws to protect our access to the sun, planners will continue as they have done and architects and builders will too.

When the Greek dramatist Aeschylus wrote about solar architecture and about people living like ants in sunless caves he presented an uncomfortably accurate allegory of life in the 21st century. This is how many of us are condemned to live. Existing lighting strategies support human vision. In future, they will need to address the biological effects of light and darkness. Much remains unknown on the subject. Based on what has been discovered already, the current approach to lighting the interior and exterior of buildings does not serve the best interests of the people inside them. A greater appreciation of natural light and, in particular, direct sunlight by designers and legislators would do a great deal to improve our safety and health in and around buildings. It would help to reduce the enormous financial and social burden on society of depression, vitamin D deficiency, infectious diseases and the recovery of hospital patients. The impact of solar access legislation on architecture and town planning would be profound. If we had a right to the sun there really would be a revolution.

References

Introduction

Nightingale F. *Notes on Hospitals.* John W. London, Parker and Son, 1859.

Nightingale F. *Notes on Nursing: What it is and What it is Not.* London, Harrison 1860.

Burberry P. *Environment and Services.* London, Batsford, Third Edition, 1977.

Chapter 1. Nothing New Under the Sun

Aretaeus, of Cappadocia. *The Extant Works of Aretaeus, the Cappadocian,* (ed. and trans. F. Adams). London, Sydenham Society, 1856.

Aurelianus C. *On Acute Diseases and on Chronic Diseases.* (trans. El Drabkin) Chicago, University of Chicago Press 1950.

Barss P, Comfort K. Ward design and jaundice in the tropics: report of an epidemic. *British Medical Journal* 1985;291:400–401.

Basta SS. Malnutrition by design. *Lancet* 1993 Apr 10;341(8850):934.

Bernhard O. *Light Treatment in Surgery.* London, Edward Arnold & Co. 1926.

Berson DM, Dunn FA, Takao M. Phototransduction by retinal ganglion cells that set the circadian clock. *Science* 8 February 2002;295(5557):1070–1073.

British Standards Institution, *Basic Data for the Design of Buildings: Sunlight, Draft for Development* DD67, BSI, 1980.

Butti K, Perlin JK. *A Golden Thread – 2500 Years of Solar Architecture and Technology.* London, Marion Boyars 1980.

Castaglioni A. *A History of Medicine.* New York, Alfred-Knoff 1941.

Cicero. *De Legibus.* Book 3, Chapter 3, Section 8.

Cremer RJ, Perryman PW, Richards DH. Influence of light on the hyper-bilirubinemia of infants. *Lancet* 1958;1:1094–1097.

Downes A, Blunt TP. Researches on the effect of light upon bacteria and other organisms. *Proc Roy Soc* 1877;26:488–500.

Downing D. *Day Light Robbery.* London, Arrow Books 1988.

Finsen N. *Phototherapy.* London, Edward Arnold 1901.

Fitzpatrick M. *The Tyranny of Health: Doctors and the Regulation of Lifestyle.* London, Routledge 2001.

Ghadioungui P (trans.) *The Ebers Papyrus.* Academy of Scientific Research. Cairo 1987.

Gillie O. *Sunlight, Vitamin D & Health.* London, Health Research Forum 2006.

Golden RN et al. The efficacy of light therapy in the treatment of mood disorders: A review and meta-analysis of the evidence. *Am J Psych* April 2005;656–62.

Gordon CM, De Peter KC, Feldman HA, et al. Prevalence of vitamin D deficiency among healthy adolescents. *Arch Pediatr Adolesc Med* 2004;158:531–7.

Hattar S, Liao M et al. Melanopsin-containing retinal ganglion cells: architecture, projections, and intrinsic photosensitivity. *Science* 8 February 2002; 295 (5557):1065–1070.

Helfand et al. "Salus Populi Suprema Lex": the health of the people is the supreme law. *Am J Public Health.* 2001;91:689.

Hickey L, Gordon CM. Vitamin D deficiency: new perspectives on an old disease. *Curr Opin Endocrinol Diabetes* 2004;11:18–25.

Hippocrates. *Works of Hippocrates.* (trans and ed. WHS Jones and ET Withington), Cambridge Mass: Harvard University Press, 1923–1931.

Hockberger PE. A history of ultraviolet photobiology for humans, animals and microorganisms. *Photochem Photobiol* 2002 Dec;76(6):561–79.

Kime ZR. *Sunlight Could Save Your Life.* California, World Health Publications 1980.

Lambert GW, Reid C, Kaye DM et al. Effect of sunlight and season on serotonin turnover in the brain. *Lancet* 2002;360:1840–1842.

Landels JG. *Engineering in the Ancient World.* California, University of California Press 2000.

Le Corbusier. *The Athens Charter* (trans. A. Eardley). New York, Grossman Publishers 1973.

McGuire L, Heffner K. et al. Pain and wound healing in surgical patients. *Ann Behav Medicine* 2006 Apr;31(2):165–72.

Nightingale F. *Notes on Hospitals.* London, Parker and Son, 1859.

Nightingale F. *Notes on Nursing; What it is and What it is Not.* New York, Dover Publications, 1969.

Nutton V. The perils of patriotism: Pliny and Roman medicine. In R French and F Greenaway (eds.) *Science in the early Roman empire: Pliny the Elder, his Sources and Influence.* Ottowa 1986.

Page JK (Ed.), *Indoor Environment: Health Aspects of Air Quality, Thermal Environment, Light and Noise,* WHO/EHE/RUD/90.2, World Health Organization, Geneva, 1990.

Pliny The Elder. *Natural History – A Selection.* (trans. J.F. Healy), London, Penguin Books, 1991.

Powers GF, Park EA, Shipley PG, McCollum EV, and Simmonds N. The prevention of the development of rickets in rats. *J Am Med Assoc* 1922;78(3)159–165.

Scarborough J. *Roman Medicine.* London, Thames & Hudson, 1969.

Scragg R, Khaw KT, Murphy S. Effect of winter oral vitamin D3 supplementation on cardiovascular risk factors in elderly adults. *Eur J Clin Nutr* 1995;49:640–46.

Sedrani SH. Low 25–hydroxyvitamin D and normal serum calcium concentrations in Saudi Arabia: Riyadh region. *Ann Nutr Metab* 1984;28:181–85.

Seneca: *Letters from a Stoic.* (trans. R.A. Campbell). London, Penguin, 1975.

Shaw B. *The Doctor's Dilemma.* London, Penguin, 1979.

Taha SA, Dost SM, Sedrani SH. 25–Hydroxyvitamin D and total calcium: extraordinarily low plasma concentrations in Saudi mothers and their neonates. *Pediatr Res* 1984;18:739–41.

Thomas MK, Demay MB. Vitamin D deficiency and disorders of vitamin D metabolism. *Endocrinol Metab Clin North Am* 2000;29:611–27.

Ulpian. *Digest.* 8.2; 17.

Vitruvius. *The Ten Books on Architecture.* (trans. M.H. Morgan), New York, Dover Publications, 1960.

Walch JM, Rabin BR, Day R et al. The effect of sunlight on postoperative analgesic medication use: a prospective study of patients undergoing spinal surgery. *Psychosomatic Med* 2005;67:156–163.

WHO. The World Health Report, World Health Organization, Geneva, 2001.

Chapter 2. Light and Your Health

Barger-Lux MJ, Heaney RP. Effects of above average summer sun exposure on serum 25–Hydroxyvitamin D and calcium absorption. *J Clin Endocrinol Metab* 2002 Nov; 87(11):4952–6.

Barinaga M. Circadian clock: how the brain's clock gets daily enlightenment. *Science* 2002 February 8th:955–957.

Beauchemin KM, Hayes P. Dying in the dark: sunshine, gender, and outcomes in Myocardial Infarction. *J Roy Soc Med* 1998;91:352–354.

Beauchemin KM, Hayes P. Sunny rooms expedite recovery from severe and refractory depressions. *J Affect Disorders* 1996;40:49–51.

Benedetti F et al. Morning sunlight reduces length of hospitalization in bipolar depression. *J Affect Disorders* 2001;62:221–223.

Berson DM, Dunn FA, Takao,M. Phototransduction by retinal ganglion cells that set the circadian clock. *Science* 8 February 2002;295(5557):1070–1073

Bizzarri M, Cucina A et al. Melatonin and vitamin D3 increase TGF-beta1 release and induce growth inhibition in breast cancer cell cultures. *J Surg Res* 2003 Apr;110(2):332–7.

Blask DE, Brainard GC et al. Melatonin-depleted blood from premenopausal women exposed to light at night stimulates growth of human breast cancer xenografts in nude rats. *Cancer Research* 2005 Dec 1;65:11174–84.

Boyce PR. *Human Factors in Lighting.* Florida, CRC Press, 2002.

Brainard GC and Hanafin JP. The effects of light on human health and behaviour: relevance to architectural lighting. Proc CIE Expert Symposium Light and Health: Non-visual Effects, Vienna, Austria, 30 September–2 October, 2004. pp 2–9.

British Standards Institution, Basic Data for the Design of Buildings: Sunlight, Draft for Development DD67, BSI, 1980.

Bullough JD, Rea MS, Figueiro MG. Of mice and women: Light as a circadian stimulus in breast cancer research. *Cancer Causes Control* 2006 May;17(4):375–383.

Cantorna MT. Vitamin D and autoimmunity: is vitamin D status an environmental factor affecting autoimmune disease prevalence? *Proc Soc Exp Biol Med* 2000;223:230–233.

Dahl K, Avery DH et al. Dim light melatonin onset and circadian temperature during a constant routine in hypersomnic winter depression, *Acta Psychiatr Scand* 1993;88:60–66.

Eagles JM. Seasonal affective disorder *Brit J Psych* 2003;182:2003.

Fetveit A, Skjerve A, Bjorvatn B. Bright light treatment improves sleep in institutionalized elderly – an open trial. *Int J Geriatr Psych* 2003;18:520–526.

Figuero MG et al. Daylight and productivity: a possible link to circadian regulation. Light and Human Health. EPRI/LRO 5th International Lighting Research Symposium, Palo Alto, CA: The Lighting Research Office of the Electric Power Research Institute, 2002. p185–193.

Figueiro MG, Bullough JD, Parsons RH, MS. Preliminary evidence for a change in spectral sensitivity of the circadian system at night. *J Circ Rhythms* 2005;3:14.

Foley DJ. Sleep complaints among elderly persons: an epidemiologic study of three communiites. *Sleep* 1995;18:425–32.

Foster R, Kreitzman L. *Rythms of Life: The Biological Clocks that Control the Daily Lives of Every Living Thing.* London, Profile Books Ltd, 2004.

Frasure-Smith et al. Depression and 18-month prognosis after myocardial infarction. *Circulation* 1995;91(4):999–1005.

Gallin PF, Terman M, Reme CE et al. Ophthalmologic examination of patients with seasonal affective disorder, before and after bright light therapy. *Am J Ophthalmol* 1995;119:202–10.

Gammack J. Effects of natural light therapy on sleep in the elderly. Proc Am Med Dirs Assoc 29th Annual Symposium March 16–19, 2006, Dallas, Texas.

Garssen J, Norval M, el Ghorr A et al. Estimation of the effect of increasing UVB exposure on the human immune system and related resistance to infectious diseases and tumours. *J Photochem Photobiol* 1998;42:167–179.

Gartner LM, Greer FR, Section on Breastfeeding and Committee on Nutrition, American Academy of Pediatrics. Prevention of rickets and vitamin D deficiency: new guidelines for vitamin D intake. *Pediatrics* 2003;111(4 pt 1):908–10.

Gillie O. *Sunlight Robbery: Health Benefits of Sunlight are Denied by Current Public Health Policy in the UK.* London, Health Research Forum, 2004.

Glerup H, Mikkelsen K et al. Commonly recommended daily intake of vitamin D is not sufficient if sunlight exposure is limited. *J Intern Med* 2000;247:260–268.

Gloth FM et al. Vitamin D deficiency in homebound elderly persons. *JAMA* 1995;274:1683–6.

Harrison Y. The relationship between daytime exposure to light and night-time sleep in 6–12-week-old infants *J Sleep Res* 2004; 13: 345–352.

Hattar S, Liao M et al. Melanopsin-containing retinal ganglion cells: architecture, projections, and intrinsic photosensitivity. *Science* 8 February 2002;295 (5557):1065–1070.

Heaney RP, Davies KM, Chen TC, Holick MF, Barger-Lux MJ. Human serum 25-hydroxycholecalciferol response to extended oral dosing with cholecalciferol. *Am J Clin Nutr* 2003 Jan;77(1):204–10.

Hickey L, Gordon CM. Vitamin D deficiency: new perspectives on an old disease. *Curr Opin End Diab* 2004;11:18–25.

Hoekstra R. Effect of light therapy on biopterin, neopterin and tryptophan in patients with seasonal affective disorder. *Psychiatry Res.* 2003 Aug 30;120(1):37–42.

Holick FM. Vitamin D: A millennium perspective. *J Cell Biochem* 2003;88:296–307.

Holick MF. The photobiology of vitamin D and its consequences for humans. *Ann New York Acad Sci* 1985;453:1–13.

Holick MF. Vitamin D: the underappreciated D-lightful hormone that is important for skeletal and cellular health. *Curr Opin Endocrinol Diab* 2002;9:87–98.

Kobayashi R, Fukada N, Kohsaka M et al. Effects of bright light at lunchtime on sleep of patients in a geriatric hospital *I. Psychiatry Clin Neurosci* 2001;55(3):287–289.

Kobayashi R, Kohsaka M, Fukuda N et al. Effects of morning bright light on sleep in healthy elderly women. *Psychiatry Clin Neurosci* 1999;53(2):237–238.

Kogan AO, Guilford PM. Side effects of short-term 10,000 lux light therapy. *Am J Psychiatry* 1998;155:293–4.

Kohsaka M, Fukuda N, Kobayashi R et al. Effects of short duration morning bright light in healthy elderly II: sleep and motor activity. *Psychaitry Clin Neurosci* 1998;52(2):252–253.

Kripke DF. Light treatment for nonseasonal depression: speed, efficacy, and combined treatment. *J Affect Disorders* 1998;49:109–1

Lambert GW, Reid C, Kaye DM, Jennings GL, Esler MD. Effect of sunlight and season on serotonin turnover in the brain. *Lancet* 2002 Dec 7;360(9348):1840–2.

Lehtonen-Veromaa M, Mottonen T, et al. Vitamin D intake is low and hypovitaminosis D common in healthy 9- to 15-year old Finnish girls. *Eur J Clin Nutr* 1999; 53(9): 74–76.

Lewy A, Wehr T, Goodwin F et al. Light suppresses melatonin secretion in humans. *Science* 1980; 210:1267–1269.

Lewy AJ, Sack RL, Miller LS, Hoban TM: Antidepressant and circadian phase-shifting effects of light. *Science* 1987; 235: 352–354.

Lockyer J Norman. *The Dawn of Astronomy.* Cambridge, MIT Press 1894.

Magnusson A. Seasonal affective disorder: an overview. *Chronobiol Int* 2003 Mar;20(2):189–207.

Mardaljevic J. Examples of climate-based daylight modelling. CIBSE National Conference 2006: Engineering the Future, Oval Cricket Ground, London, 21–22 March 2006.

Mezquita-Raya P, Munoz-Torres M, De Dios Luna J, et al. Relation between vitamin D insufficiency, bone density, and bone metabolism in healthy postmenopausal women. *J Bone Miner Res* 2001;16:1408–15.

Muldoon MF et al. Blunted central serotonergic responsivity is associated with preclinical vascular disease. Proc. 64th Annual Scientific Conference of the American Psychosomatic Society, Denver, Colorado, March 1-4, 2006.

Muller K, Bendtzen K. 1,25-Dihydroxyvitamin D3 as a natural regulator of human immune functions. *J Investig Dermatol Symp Proc* 1996;1:68–71.

National Radiological Protection Board. Report of the Advisory Group on Non-ionising Radiation (AGNIR): Effects of ultraviolet radiation on human health. Documents of the NRPB 2002;13(1).

Nemerhoff CB et al. Depression and cardiac disease. *Depress Anxiety* 1998;8:71–9.

Nightingale F. *Notes on Nursing; What it is and What it is Not.* New York, Dover Publications 1969.

Norris D, Tillet L. Daylight and productivity: is there a causal link? Proc Glass Processing Days Conference: Tampere, Finland, 1997. p213–218.

Outila TA, Karkkainen MU, Seppanen RH, Lamberg-Allardt CJ. Dietary intake of vitamin D in premenopausal, healthy vegans was insufficient to maintain concentrations of serum 25- hydroxyvitamin D and intact parathyroid hormone within normal ranges during the winter in Finland. *J Am Diet Assoc* 2000;100(4):434–41.

Park EA. The therapy of rickets. *JAMA* 1940;115(5):370–9.

Partonen T, Lonnqvist J. Seasonal affective disorder. *Lancet* 1998;352:1369–74.

Pauley SM. Lighting for the human circadian clock: recent research indicates that lighting has become a public health issue. *Medl Hypoth* 2004; 63 (4): 588–596.

Plehwe WE. Vitamin D deficiency in the 21st century: an unnecessary pandemic? *Clin Endocrinol* 2003 Jul;59(1):22–4.

Ponsonby AL, McMichael M, van der Mei I. Ultraviolet radiation and autoimmune disease: insights from epidemiological research. *Toxicology* 2002;181-182:71–78.

Rea MS. Light - much more than vision? Light and Human Health: EPRI/LRO 5th International Lighting Research Symposium. Palo Alto, CA: The Lighting Research Office of the Electric Power Research Institute, 2002. p1–15.

Rea MS, Figueiro MG, Bullough, JD. Circadian photobiology: An emerging framework for lighting practice and research. *Ltg Res and Tech* 2002;34(3):177–190.

Reinhard CF, Voss K. Monitoring manual control of electric lighting and blinds *Ltg Res and Tech* 2003; 35:243–260.

Richardson JP. Vitamin D deficiency – the once and present epidemic. *Am Fam Physician* 2005 Jan 15;71(2):241–2.

Rosenthal NE, et al. Seasonal affective disorder: a description of the syndrome and preliminary findings with light therapy. *Arch Gen Psychiatry* 1984; 41:72–80.

Saeed AS, Bruce TJ. Seasonal affective disorders. *Am Fam Phys* 1998;57:1340–9.

Semba RD, Garrett E, Johnson BA, et al. Vitamin D deficiency among older women with and without disability. *Am J Clin Nutr* 2000;72:1529–34.

Schernhammer ES, Hankinson SE. Urinary melatonin levels and breast cancer risk. *J National Cancer Inst* 2005 July 20:2005;1084–7.

Schernhammer ES et al. Night work and risk of breast cancer. *Epidemiol* 2006 Jan:108-11.

Schuster S. Sun and the Skin: Violation of Truth, in S Feldman, V Marks (eds.) *Panic Nation: Unpicking the Myths We're told about Food and Health.* London, John Blake Publishing Ltd 2005.

Schwartz GG, Blot WJ. Vitamin d status and cancer incidence and mortality: Something new under the sun. *J Natl Cancer Inst* 2006;98(7):428–30.

Stumpf WE, Sar M, Reid FA, Tanaka Y, DeLuca HF. Target cells for 1,25-dihydroxyvitamin D3 in intestinal tract, stomach, kidney, skin, pituitary, and parathyroid. *Science* 1979;20:1188–90.

Taylor CB, Youngblood ME et al. Effects of antidepressant medication on morbidity and mortality in depressed patients after myocardial infarction. *Arch Gen Psychiatry* 2005 Jul;62(7):711–2.

Trivedi DP, Doll R, Khaw KT. Effect of four monthly oral vitamin D3 (cholecalciferol) supplementation on fractures and mortality in men and women living in the community: randomised double blind controlled trial. *BMJ* 2003;326:469.

Thomas MK, Lloyd-Jones DM, Thadhani RI et al. Hypovitaminosis D in medical inpatients. *N Engl J Med* 1998;338:777–83.

Veith R, Cole DE, Hawker GA et al. Wintertime vitamin D insufficiency is common in young Canadian women, and their vitamin D intake does not prevent it. *Eur J Clin Nutr* 2001; 55:1091–7.

Veith R. Vitamin D supplementation, 25-hydroxyvitamin D and safety. *Am J Clin Nutr* 1999;69:842–56.

Veith R, Fraser D. Vitamin D insufficiency: no recommended dietary allowance exists for this nutrient. *Can Med Assoc J* 2002;166(12):1541–1542.

Vieth R. Why the optimal requirement for vitamin D3 is probably much higher than what is officially recommended for adults. *J Steroid Biochem and Mol Biol* 2004;89-90: 575–579.

Verkasalo PK et al. Sleep duration and breast cancer: A prospective cohort study. *Cancer Research* 2005 Oct 15;17:9595–9600.

Wehr TA. Seasonal affective disorder: a historical overview. In NE Rosenthal and ME Blehar (Eds.) *Seasonal Affective Disorders and Phototherapy.* New York, Guildford Press1989.

Wehr TA, Rosenthal NE. Seasonality and affective illness. *Am J Psychiatry* 1989 Jul;146(7):829–839.

Chapter 3. Depressed? You soon will be

Altmeyer P, Stohr L, Holzman H. Seasonal rhythm of the plasma level of alpha-melanocyte stimulating hormone. *J Invest Dermatol* 1986;86:454–6.

Arunabh S, Pollack S, Yeh J, Aloia JF. Body fat content and 25-hydroxyvitamin D levels in healthy women. *J Clin Endocrinol Metab* 2003 Jan;88(1):157–61.

Avery DH, Kizer D, Bolte MA, Hellekson C. Bright light therapy of subsyndromal seasonal affective disorder in the workplace: morning vs. afternoon exposure. *Acta Psychiatr Scand* 2001; 103(4):267–274.

Babyak M, Blumenthal JA et al. Exercise treatment for major depression: maintenance of therapeutic benefit at 10 months. *Psychosom Med* 2000;62(5):633–638.

Bell NH et al. Evidence for alteration of the vitamin D-endocrine system in obese subjects. *J.Clin.Invest* 1985;76:370–3.

Blumenthal JA, Babyak MA et al. Effects of exercise training on older patients with major depression. *Arch Intern Med* 1999;159(19):2349–2356.

Boucher BJ. Inadequate vitamin D status: does it contribute to the disorders comprising syndrome 'X'? *Br J Nutr* 1998;79:315–27.

Buffington C et al. Vitamin D deficiency in the morbidly obese. *Obes Surg* 1993;3:421–4.

Chaouloff F. Physical exercise and brain monoamines: a review. *Acta Physiol Scand* 1989 Sep;137(1):1–13.

Deisenhammer EA. Weather and suicide: the present state of knowledge on the association of meteorological factors with suicidal behaviour. *Acta Psychiatr Scand* 2003;108:402–409.

Dunn AL et al. The DOSE study: a clinical trial to examine efficacy and dose response of exercise as treatment for depression. *Control Clin Trials* 2002;23(5):584–603.

Eagles JM. Light therapy and the management of winter depression. *Advan Psych Treat* 2004;10: 233–240.

Eagles JM. Seasonal affective disorder. *Brit J Psych* 2003;182:174–176.

Eastman CI, Hoese EK, Youngstedt SD, Liu L. Phase-shifting human circadian rhythms with exercise during the night shift. *Physiol Behav* 1995;58(6):1287–1291.

Espiritu RC et al. Low illumination experienced by San Diego adults: association with atypical depressive symptoms. *Biol Psych* 1994 March 15;35(6):403–407

Fehm H et al. The melanocortin melanocyte-stimulating hormone/adrenocorticotropin(4-10) decreases body fat in humans. *J Clin Endocrinol and Metab* 2001;86(3):1144–47.

Feldman S, Marks V. *Panic Nation: Unpicking the Myths We're told about Food and Health.* London, John Blake Publishing Ltd, 2005.

Fitzpatrick M. *The Tyranny of Health: Doctors and the Regulation of Lifestyle.* London, Routledge, 2001.

Ford ES, Ajani UA, McGuire LC, Liu S. Concentrations of serum vitamin D and the metabolic syndrome among U.S. adults. *Diabetes Care* 2005 May;28(5):1228–30.

Frank LD, Andresen MA, Schmid TL. Obesity relationships with community design, physical activity, and time spent in cars. *Am J Prev Med* 2004;27(2):87–96.

Freudenberg N. Time for a national agenda to improve the health of urban populations. *Am J Public Health* 2000;90:837–840.

Friedrich MJ. Epidemic of obesity expands its spread to developing countries. *JAMA* 2002;287:1382–6.

Gallin PF, Terman M, Reme CE, et al. Ophthalmologic examination of patients with seasonal affective disorder, before and after bright light therapy. *Am J Ophthalmol* 1995;119:202–10.

Gloth F, Alam W, Hollis B. Vitamin D vs broad spectrum phototherapy in the treatment of seasonal affective disorder. *Nutr Health Aging* 1999;3(1):5–7.

Golden RN et al. The efficacy of light therapy in the treatment of mood disorders: a review and meta-analysis of the evidence. *Am J Psychiatry* 2005;162:656–662.

Greden JF. The burden of recurrent depression: causes consequences and future prospects. *J Clin Psych* 2001;62(suppl 22):5–9.

Hang S, et al. 1-alpha,25-dihydroxyvitamin D3 modulates human adipocyte metabolism via nongenomic action. *The FASEB Journal* 2001;15:2751–53.

Heisler et al. Serotonin reciprocally regulates melanocortin neurons to modulate food Intake. *Neuron* 2006 July 20;51,239–249.

Hibbeln JR, Salem N. Dietary polyunsaturated fats and depression: when cholesterol does not satisfy. *Am J Clin Nutr* 1995;62:1–9.

Hibbeln JR. Fish consumption and major depression. *Lancet* 1998;351:1213.

House of Commons. Obesity. House of Commons Health Committee 3rd Report of Session 2003–04, Volume I. London, HMSO 2004.

House of Commons. The Influence of the Pharmaceutical Industry. House of Commons Health Committee. 4th Report of Session 2004–05 Volume I. London, HMSO 2005.

Jorde R, Waterloo K, Saleh F, Haug E, Svartberg J. Neuropsychological function in relation to serum parathyroid hormone and serum 25-hydroxyvitamin D levels The Tromso study. *J Neurol* 2006 Apr;253(4):464–70.

Kamycheva E, Joakimsen R, Jorde R. Intakes of calcium and vitamin D predict body mass index in the population of northern Norway. *J Nutr* 2002; 132:102–6.

Klerman GL, Weissman MM. Increasing rates of depression. *JAMA* 1989;261:2229–35.

Klerman GL. The current age of youthful melancholia. Evidence for increase in depression among adolescents and young adults. *Br J Psych* 1988;152:4–14.

Kogan AO, Guilford PM. Side effects of short-term 10,000 lux light therapy. *Am J Psychiatry* 1998;155:293–4.

Kripke, D. F. Light Treatment for nonseasonal depression: speed, efficacy, and combined treatment. *J Affective Disord* 1998;49:109–117.

Lambert G, Reid C, Kaye D, Jennings G, Esler M. Increased suicide rate in the middle-aged and its association with hours of sunlight. *Am J Psychiatry.* 2003 Apr;160(4):793–5.

Lansdowne A, Provost S. Vitamin D3 enhances mood in healthy subjects during winter. Psychopharm 1998;135(4):319-23.

Lawlor DA, Hopker SW. The effectiveness of exercise as an intervention in the management of depression: systematic review and meta-regression analysis of randomised controlled trials. *BMJ* 2001;322(7289):763–767.

Leppämäki S, Partonen T et al. Timed bright-light exposure and complaints related to shift work among women. *Scand J Work Environ Health* 2003;29(1):22–26.

Leppämäki S, Partonen T, Lönnqvist J. Bright-light exposure combined with physical exercise elevates mood. *J Affect Disord* 2002;72(2):139–144.

Liel Y et al. Low circulating vitamin D in obesity. *Calcif Tissue Int* 1988;43:199–201.

Liu S et al. Dietary Calcium, Vitamin D, and the prevalence of metabolic syndrome in middle-aged and older U.S. women. *Diabetes Care* 2005;28:2926–32.

Logan AC. Omega-3 fatty acids and major depression: A primer for the mental health professionals. *Lipids Health Dis* 2004;3:25.

Macintyre S. The social patterning of exercise behaviours: the role of personal and local resources *Br J Sports Med* 2000; 34:6.

Maidment ID. Are fish oils an effective therapy in mental illness?-an analysis of the data. *Acta Psychiatr Scand* 2000;102:3–11.

Miller AL. Epidemiology, etiology, and natural treatment of seasonal affective disorder. *Alt Med Rev* 2005 March; 5–13.

Mokdad AH et al. The continuing epidemics of obesity and diabetes in the United States. *JAMA* 2001;286:1195–200.

Mokdad AH et al. The spread of the obesity epidemic in the United States, 1991–1998. *JAMA* 1999;282:1519–22.

Moynihan R, Cassels A. *Selling Sickness: How the World's Pharmaceutical Companies Are Turning Us All Into Patients.* New York, Nation Books 2005.

Musselman DL, Evans DL, Nemeroff CB. The relationship of depression to cardiovascular disease: epidemiology, biology, and treatment. *Arch Gen Psychiatry* 1998;55(7):580–592.

Obradovic D, Gronemeyer H, Lutz B, Rein T. Cross-talk of vitamin D and glucocorticoids in hippocampal cells. *J Neurochem.* 2006 Jan;96(2):500–9.

Papadopoulos F, Frangakis C et al. A role of sunshine in triggering suicide. *Epidemiology* 2002;13(4):492–3.

Papadopoulos FC, Frangakis CE et al. Exploring lag and duration effect of sunshine in triggering suicide. *J Affect Disord* 2005 Nov;88(3):287–97.

Partonen T, Leppämäki S, Hurme J, Lönnqvist J. Randomized trial of physical exercise alone or combined with bright light on mood and health-related quality of life. *Psychol Med* 1998; 28(6):1359–1364.

Partonen T, Lonnqvist J. Bright light improves vitality and alleviates distress in healthy people. *J Affect Disord* 2000 Jan–Mar;57(1-3):55–61.

Partonen T. Vitamin D and serotonin in winter. *Med Hypothesis* 1998 Sep;51(3):267–8.

Schwartz, M. Progress in the search for neuronal mechanisms coupling type 2 diabetes to obesity. *J Clin Invest* 2001;108: 963–4.

Scott J, Dickey B. Global burden of depression: the intersection of culture and medicine *Brit J Psych* 2003;183:92–94.

Shaw K, Turner J, Del Mar C. Tryptophan and 5-hydroxytryptophan for depression (Cochrane Review). In: The Cochrane Library, Issue 4, 2001.

Stoll AL et al. Omega 3 fatty acids in bipolar disorder: a preliminary double-blind, placebo-controlled trial. *Arch Gen Psychiatry* 1999;56:407–412.

Stoner SC et al. RW. Psychiatric comorbidity and medical illness. *Med Update Psych* 1998;3(3):64–70.

Terman M, Terman JS. Light therapy for seasonal and nonseasonal depression: Efficacy, protocol, safety, and side effects. *CNS Spectrums* August 2005;647–63.

Thomas CM, Morris S. Cost of depression among adults in England in 2000. *Brit J Psych* 2003;183:515–519.

Treffers PD, Rinne-Albers MA.Selective serotonin reuptake inhibitors (SSRI's) are not indicated for children and adolescents with depression. *Nederlands Ned Tijdschr Geneeskd* 2005 Jun 11;149(24):1314–7 [Article in Dutch]

Vandegrift D, Yoked T. Obesity rates, income, and suburban sprawl: an analysis of US states. *Health Place* 2004 Sep;10(3):221–9.

Whittington CJ et al. Selective serotonin reuptake inhibitors in childhood depression: systematic review of published versus unpublished data. *Lancet* 2004 Apr 24;363:1341–45.

WHO Consultation on Obesity. Obesity: preventing and managing the global epidemic. WHO Technical Report Series 894. Geneva, Switzerland: World Health Organization; 2000.

Wirz-Justice A, Graw P et al. 'Natural' light treatment of seasonal affective disorder. *J Affect Disord* 1996;37(2-3):109–120.

Wirz-Justice A, et al. Chronotherapeutics (light and wake therapy) in affective disorders. *Psychol Med* 2005 July;939–44.

Wortsman J et al., Decreased bioavailability of vitamin D in obesity. *Am J Clin Nutr* 2000;72:690–3.

Wurtman RJ, Wurtman JJ. Brain serotonin, carbohydrate-craving, obesity and depression. *Obesity Research* 1995;3:477S–480S.

Chapter 4. Vitamin D Deficiency 'The Silent Epidemic'

Abrams SA. Nutritional rickets: an old disease returns. *Nutr Rev* 2002;60:111–115.

Al Faraj S, Al Mutairi K. Vitamin D deficiency and chronic low back pain in Saudi Arabia. *Spine* 2003 Jan 15;28(2):177–9.

Allain TJ, Dhesi J. Hypovitaminosis d in older adults. *Gerontology* 2003 Sep–Oct;49(5):273–8.

Altschul R and Herman HI. Ultraviolet irradiation and cholesterol metabolism. Seventh Annual Meeting of The American Society for the Study of Atherosclerosis. *Circulation* 1953;8:438.

Amento EP Bhalla AK Kurnick JT et al. 1 alpha,25-dihydroxyvitamin D3 induces maturation of the human monocyte cell line U937, and, in association with a factor from human T lymphocytes, augments production of the monokine, mononuclear cell factor. *J Clin Invest* 1984;73:731–739.

American Academy of Pediatrics Committee on Environmental Health. Ultraviolet light: a hazard to children. *Pediatrics* 1999;104:(2)328–332.

Angwafo FF. Migration and prostate cancer: an international perspective. *J Natl Med Assoc* 1998;90(11 suppl):S720–723.

Anon, Nutrition and bone health: with particular reference to calcium and vitamin D. Department of Health report on health and social subjects No. 49. London, HMSO. 1998.

Anon. Coronary heart disease statistics. British Heart Foundation Database. (wwwheartstats.com)

Anon. How much is too much? We can't ignore new evidence that a little sunlight does you good. *New Scientist* 2003 August 9;3.

Apperley FL. The relation of solar radiation to cancer mortality in North America. *Cancer Res* 1941;1:191–196.

Atik OS, Gunal I, Korkusuz F. Burden of osteoporosis. *Clin Orthop Relat Res* 2006 Feb;443:19–24.

Barger-Lux MJ, Heaney RP. Effects of above average summer sun exposure on serum 25-Hydroxyvitamin D and calcium absorption. *J Clin Endocrinol Metab* 2002 Nov; 87(11):4952–56.

Bellamy R. Evidence of a gene-environment interaction in development of tuberculosis. *Lancet* 2000;355:588–589.

Berwick M. et al. Sun exposure and mortality from melanoma. *J Nat Cancer Inst* 2005 February 2;97;3:195–198

Black HS et al. Effect of a low-fat diet on the incidence of actinic keratosis. *N Engl J Med* 1994 May 5;330(18):1272–5.

Black HS. Influence of dietary factors on actinically-induced skin cancer. *Mutat Res* 1998 Nov 9;422(1):185–90.

Blank S, Scanlon KS, Sinks TH, Lett S, Falk H. An outbreak of hypervitaminosis D associated with the overfortification of milk from a home-delivery dairy. *Am J Public Health* 1995;85(5):656–659.

Boucher B. Sunlight 'D' ilemma. *Lancet* 2001;357:961.

Brookes GB. Vitamin D deficiency – a new cause of cochlear deafness. *J Laryngol Otol.* 1983 May;97(5):405–20.

Brookes GB. Vitamin D deficiency and deafness: 1984 update. *Am J Otol* 1985 Jan;6(1):102–7.

Burleigh E, Potter J. Vitamin D deficiency in outpatients: a Scottish perspective. *Scott Med J* 2006 May;51(2):27–31.

Calvo MS, Whiting SJ. Prevalence of vitamin D insufficiency in Canada and the United States: importance to health status and efficacy of current food fortification and dietary supplement use. *Nutr Rev* 2003 Mar;61(3):107–13.

Cantorna MT. Vitamin D and autoimmunity: is vitamin D status an environmental factor affecting autoimmune disease prevalence? *Proc Soc Exp Biol Med* 2000;223:230–233.

Carter AJ. A Christmas Carol: Charles Dickens and the birth of orthopaedics. *J R Soc Med* 1993 Jan;86(1):45–8.

Cauvin JF. *Des Bienfaits de l'Insolation.* Ph.D. Thesis, University of Paris, France 1815.

Chan TY. Vitamin D deficiency and susceptibility to tuberculosis. *Calcif Tissue Int* 2000;66(6):476–478.

Christophers AJ. Melanoma is not caused by sunlight. *Mutat Res* 1998 Nov 9;422(1):113–7.

Danielsson C, Torma H et al. Positive and negative interaction of 1,25-dihydroxyvitamin D3 and the retinold CD437 in the induction of human cell apoptosis. *Int J Cancer* 1999;81:467–470.

Das, G et al. Hypovitaminosis D among healthy adolescent girls attending an inner city school. *Arch Dis Child* 2006 Jul;91(7):569–72.

Davies PD. A possible link between vitamin D deficiency and impaired host defense to Mycobacterium tuberculosis. *Tubercle* 1995;66:301–306.

Di Tano G, Picerno I, et al. Chlamydia pneumoniae and Helicobacter pylori infections in acute myocardial infarction. *Ital Heart J* 2000;1(12 Suppl):1576–81.

Dickens C. *The Life and Adventures of Nicholas Nickleby.* London, The Gresham Publishing Company, 1904.

Douglas AS, Shaukat A, Bakhshi SS. Does vitamin D deficiency account for ethnic differences in tuberculosis seasonality in the UK? *Ethnicity and Health* 1998;3:247–253.

Downing D. Vitamin D – time for reassessment. *J Nutr Env Med* 2001;11:237–239.

Drew T et al. Solar forcing of regional climate change during the Maunder Minimum. *Science* 2001 7th Dec;294(5549);2149–52.

Du X, Greenfield H, Fraser DR, et al. Vitamin D deficiency and associated factors in adolescent girls in Beijing. *Am J Clin Nutr* 2001;74:494–500.

Dunn PM. Professor Armand Trousseau (1801–67) and the treatment of rickets. *Arch Dis Fetal Neonatal Ed* 1999;80:F155–F157.

Egan KM, Sosman JA, Blot WJ. Sunlight and reduced risk of cancer: is the real story vitamin D? *J Natl Cancer Inst* 2005 Feb 2;97(3):161–3.

Ekstrom K. et al. Ultraviolet radiation exposure and risk of malignant lymphomas. *J Nat Cancer Inst* 2005;97(3):199–209.

Elwood JM. Melanoma and sun exposure: contrasts between intermittent and chronic exposure. *World Journal of Surgery* 1992;16(2):157–65.

Eriksen EF, Glerup H. Vitamin D deficiency and aging: implications for general health and osteoporosis. *Biogerontology* 2002;3(1–2):73–7.

Evans SRT Houghton AM et al. Vitamin D receptor and growth inhibition by 1,25-dihydroxyvitamin D3 in human malignant melanoma cell lines. *J Surg Res* 1996;61:127–133.

Feldman S, Marks V. *Panic Nation: Unpicking the Myths We're told about Food and Health.* London, John Blake Publishing Ltd, 2005.

Feskanich D, et al. Calcium, vitamin D, milk consumption, and hip fractures: a prospective study among postmenopausal women. *Am J Clin Nutr* 2003;77(2):504–511.

Findlay L et al. A Study of Social and Economic Factors in the Causation of Rickets. Medical Research Committee Special Report 20. Galston and Sons. London. 1918.

Fraser AG, Scragg RK, Cox B, Jackson RT. Helicobacter pylori, Chlamydia pneumoniae and myocardial infarction. *Intern Med J* 2003;33(7):267–72.

Freedman DM et al. Sunlight and mortality from breast, ovarian, colon, prostate, and non-melanoma skin cancer: a composite death certificate based case-control study. *Occup Environ Med* 2002;59(4):257–262.

Fry A, Verne J. Editorial. *BMJ* 2003;326:114–115.

Fuller KE, Casparian JM. Vitamin D: balancing cutaneous and systemic considerations. *South Med J* 2001;94(1):58–64.

Garland CF et al. The role of vitamin D in cancer prevention. *Am J Public Health* 2006 Feb;96(2)252–261.

Garssen J, Norval M, el Ghorr A et al. Estimation of the effect of increasing UVB exposure on the human immune system and related resistance to infectious diseases and tumours. *J Photochem Photobiol* 1998;42:167–179.

Gillie O. *Sunlight Robbery.* Health Research Forum, London.

Giovannucci E. The epidemiology of vitamin D and cancer incidence and mortality: A review (United States). *Cancer Causes Control.* 2005 Mar;16(2):83–95.

Giovanucci E, et al. Prospective study of predictors of vitamin d status and cancer incidence and mortality amongst men. *J Nat Cancer Inst* 2006;98(7):451–459.

Glerup H, Mikkelsen K et al. Commonly recommended daily intake of vitamin D is not sufficient if sunlight exposure is limited. *J Intern Med* 2000;247:260–268.

Glisson F. *De Rachitide sive Morbo puerili, qui vulgo.* The Rickets Diciteur. London. 1650.

Glisson F. *Treatise of the Rickets being a Disease common to Children.* London. 1668.

Gorham ED et al. Vitamin D and prevention of colorectal cancer. *J Steroid Biochem Mol Biol* 2005;97(1–2):179–94.

Grant WB, Garland CF. The association of solar ultraviolet B (UVB) with reducing risk of cancer: multifactorial ecologic analysis of geographic variation in age-adjusted cancer mortality rates. *Anticancer Research.* 2006;26:2687–2700.

Grant WB, Garland CF, Holick MF. Comparisons of estimated economic burdens due to Insufficient solar ultraviolet irradiance and vitamin D and excess solar UV irradiance for the United States. *Photochem Photobiol.* 2005 Nov–Dec;81(6):1276–86.

Grant WB, Garland CF. A critical review of studies on vitamin D in relation to colorectal cancer. *Nutr Cancer* 2004;48:115–23.

Grant WB, Holick MF. Benefits and requirements of vitamin D for optimal health: a review. *Altern Med Rev* 2005;10:94–111.

Grant WB. An ecologic study of dietary and solar UV-B links to breast cancer mortality rates. *Cancer* 2002;94:272–81.

Grant WB. An estimate of premature cancer mortality in the U.S. Due to inadequate doses of solar ultraviolet-B radiation. *Cancer* 2002;94:1867–75.

Grant WB. Geographic variation of prostate cancer mortality rates in the United States: Implications for prostate cancer risk related to vitamin D. *Int J Cancer* 2004;111:470–71.

Grant WB. Lower vitamin-D production from solar ultraviolet-B irradiance may explain some differences in cancer survival rates. *J Natl Med Assoc* 2006;98(3):357–64.

Grimes DS et al. Sunlight, cholesterol and coronary heart disease. *Quarterly J Med* 1996;89:579–89.

Guy RA. The history of cod liver oil as a remedy. *Am J Dis Child.* 1923;26:112–116.

Hardy A. Rickets and the rest: child-care, diet and the infectious children's diseases, 1850–1914. *Soc Hist Med* 1992 5(3):389–412.

Harris RB, Foote JA, Hakim IA, Bronson DL, Alberts DS. Fatty acid composition of red blood cell membranes and risk of squamous cell carcinoma of the skin. *Cancer Epidemiol Biomarkers Prev* 2005 Apr;14(4):906–12.

Hayes CE. Nutritional management of rheumatoid arthritis: a review of the evidence. *J Hum Nutr* 2003;16(2):97–109.

Hayes CE, Nashold FE, Spach KM, Pedersen LB. The immunological functions of the vitamin D endocrine system. *Cell Mol Biol* 2003 Mar;49(2):277–300.

Heaney RP Davies KM Chen TC Holick MF and Barger-Lux MJ. Human serum 25-hydroxycholecalciferol response to extended oral dosing with cholecalciferol. *Am J Clin Nutr* 2003;77(1):204–210.

Heaney RP. Functional indices of vitamin D status and ramifications of vitamin D deficiency. *Am J Clin Nutr* 2004;80(6 Suppl):1706S–9S.

Hess AF and Unger LJ. The cure of infantile rickets by sunlight. *J Am Med Assoc* 1921;77(1):39.

Hess AF. *Rickets.* London, Henry Kimpton, 1930.

Hildebolt CF. Effect of vitamin D and calcium on periodontitis. *J Periodontol* 2005 Sep;76(9):1576–87

Hinds MW. Nonsolar factors in the epidemiology of malignant melanoma. *Nat Cancer Inst Monogr* 1992;62:173–178.

Holick FM. Vitamin D: A millennium perspective. *J Cell Biochem* 2003; 88: 296–307.

Holick MF. Sunlight 'D' ilemma: risk of skin cancer or bone disease and muscle weakness. *Lancet* 2001;357:4–5.

Holick MF. Sunlight and vitamin D for bone health and prevention of autoimmune diseases, cancers, and cardiovascular disease. *Am J Clin Nutr* 2004 Dec;80(6 Suppl):1678S–88S.

Holick MF. The vitamin D epidemic and its health consequences. *J Nutr* 2005;135(11): 2739S–48S.

Holick MF. Vitamin D: importance in the prevention of cancers, type 1 diabetes, heart disease, and osteoporosis. *Am J Clin Nutr* 2004 Mar;79(3):362–71.

Hollis B. Editorial: The determination of circulating 25-hydroxyvitamin D: no easy task. *J Clin End and Metab* 2004;89:3149–3151.

Hollis BW, Wagner CL. Vitamin D deficiency during pregnancy: an ongoing epidemic. *Am J Clin Nutr* 2006 August 1;84(2):273.

Hoyt DV, Schatten KH. *The Role of the Sun in Climate Change.* Oxford University Press, 1997.

Hyponnen E et al. Intake of vitamin D and risk of type 1 diabetes: a birth-cohort study. *Lancet* 2001;358:1500–1503.

Javaid MK et al. Maternal vitamin D status during pregnancy and childhood bone mass at age 9 years: a longitudinal study. *Lancet* 2006 Jan 7;367(9504):36–43

John EM et al. Vitamin D and breast cancer risk: The NHANES I epidemiologic follow-up study, 1971–1975 to 1992. *Cancer Epidem Bio Prevent* 1999;8:399–406.

Johnson JR et al. The effect of carbon arc radiation on blood pressure and cardiac output. *Am J Physiol* 1935;114:594–602.

Jones G, Dwyer T. Bone mass in prepubertal children: gender differences and the role of physical activity and sunlight exposure. *J Clin Endocrinol Metab* 1998 Dec;83(12):4274–9.

Karnauchau PN. Melanoma and sun exposure. [letter] *Lancet* 1995;346:915.

Krause R, Buhring M, Hopfenmuller W, Holick MF, Sharma AM. Ultraviolet B and blood pressure. [letter] *Lancet* 1998;352:709–10.

Keen RW. Burden of osteoporosis and fractures. *Curr Osteoporos Rep* 2003 Sep;1(2):66–70.

Koyama T et al. Anticoagulant effects of 1alpha, 25-Dihydroxyvitamin D3 on human myelogenous leukemia cells and monocytes. *Blood* 1998 July 1;92(1):160–167.

Krall EA. Osteoporosis and the risk of tooth loss. *Clin Calcium* 2006 Feb;16(2):63–6.

Kreiter SR, Schwartz RP, Kirkman HN Jr, et al. Nutritional rickets in African American breast-fed infants. *J Pediatr* 2000;137:153–157.

LeBoff MS, Kohlmeier L et al. Occult vitamin D deficiency in postmenopausal US women with acute hip fracture *JAMA* 1999;281:1505–1511.

Lehtonen-Veromaa M, Mottonen T, et al. Vitamin D intake is low and hypovitaminosis D common in healthy 9- to 15-year old Finnish girls. *Eur J Clin Nutr* 1999 ;53(9):74–76.

Liu PT, et al. Toll-like receptor triggering of a vitamin D-mediated human antimicrobial Response. *Science* 2006;311(5768):1770–1773.

Loomis WF. Rickets. *Scientific American* 1970;223:77–97.

Lucas R, McMichael T, Smith W, Armstrong B. Solar Ultraviolet Radiation: Global Burden of Disease from Solar Ultraviolet Radiation. Environmental Burden of Disease Series, No. 13. Geneva, World Health Organization Public Health and the Environment 2006.

Luscombe CJ et al. Exposure to ultraviolet radiation: association with susceptibility and age at presentation with prostate cancer. *Lancet* 2001;358:641–42.

Martineau AR et al. Effect of vitamin D supplementation on anti-mycobacterial immunity: a double-blind randomised placebo-controlled trial in London tuberculosis contacts. *Int J Tuberculosis Lung Dis* 2005;9(11 suppl 1):S173.

Martineau AR et al. Vitamin D status of tuberculosis patients and healthy blood donors in Samara City, Russia. *Int J Tuberculosis Lung Dis* 2005;(11 suppl 1):S225.

McCaffree J. Rickets on the rise. *J Am Diet Assoc* 2001;101(1):16–7.

Mezquita-Raya P, Munoz-Torres M, De Dios Luna J, et al. Relation between vitamin D insufficiency, bone density, and bone metabolism in healthy postmenopausal women. *J Bone Miner Res* 2001;16:1408–15.

Millen AE et al. Diet and melanoma in a case-control study. *Cancer Epidemiol Biomarkers Prev* 2004 Jun;13(6):1042–51.

Moan J et al. Solar radiation, vitamin D and survival rate of colon cancer in Norway. *J Photochem Photobiol* 2005;78 (3):189–93.

Mozolowski W. Jedrez Sniadecki (1768-1838) on the cure of rickets. *Nature* 1939;143: 121–23.

Muller K and Bendtzen K. 1,25-Dihydroxyvitamin D3 as a natural regulator of human immune functions. *J Investig Dermatol Symp Proc* 1996;1:68–71.

Ness AR et al. Are we really dying for a tan? *BMJ* 1999;319:114–116.

Nowson CA and Margerison C. Vitamin D intake and vitamin D status in Australians. *Med J Aust* 2002;177:149–152.

Nursyam EW, Amin Z, and Rumende CM. The effect of vitamin d as supplementary treatment in patients with moderately advanced pulmonary tuberculous lesion. *Acta Med Indones* 2006 Jan–Mar;38(1):3–5.

Outila TA, Karkkainen MU, Seppanen RH, Lamberg-Allardt CJ. Dietary intake of vitamin D in premenopausal, healthy vegans was insufficient to maintain concentrations of serum 25-hydroxyvitamin D and intact parathyroid hormone within normal ranges during the winter in Finland. *J Am Diet Assoc* 2000 Apr;100(4):434–41.

Pal BR, Shaw NJ. Rickets resurgence in the United Kingdom: Improving antenatal management in Asians. *J Pediatr* 2001;139(2):337–8.

Palm TA. The geographical distribution and aetiology of rickets. *Practitioner* 1890; 45: 270–90.

Park EA. The therapy of rickets *JAMA* 1940;115(5):370–379.

Peller S and Stephenson CS. Skin irradiation and cancer in the US Navy. *Am J Med Sci* 1936;194:326–333.

Peller S. Carcogenesis as a means of reducing cancer mortality. *Lancet* 1936;2:552–56

Pettifor JM. Rickets. *Calcif Tissue Int* 2002;70:398–399.

Pillow JJ, Forrest PJ, Rodda CP. Vitamin D deficiency in infants and young children born to migrant parents. *J Paediatr Child Health* 1995;31:180–184.

Plehwe WE. Vitamin D deficiency in the 21st century: an unnecessary pandemic? *Clin Endocrinol* 2003 Jul;59(1):22–4.

Ponsonby AL et al. Ultraviolet radiation and autoimmune disease: insights from epidemiological research. *Toxicology* 2002;181–182:71–78.

Poole KES et al. Reduced vitamin D in acute stroke. *Stroke* 2006;37(1):243.

Prabhala A, Garg R, Dandona P. Severe myopathy associated with vitamin D deficiency in western New York. *Arch Intern Med* 2000;160:1199–1203.

Reichrath J, Querings K. Vitamin D deficiency during pregnancy: a risk factor not only for fetal growth and bone metabolism but also for correct development of the fetal immune system? *Am J Clin Nutr* 2005;81:1177–78.

Rennie KL, Hughes J, Lang R, Jebb SA. Vitamin D: a natural inhibitor of multiple sclerosis. *Proc Nutr Soc* 2000;59(4):531–535.

Report of an Advisory Group on Non-ionising Radiation 13: (1) Health Effects of Ultraviolet Radiation. National Radiological Protection Board, Didcot, Oxfordshire. 2002.

Robinson, PD et al. The re-emerging burden of rickets: a decade of experience from Sydney. *Arch Dis Child* 2006;91:564–568.

Robsahm TE, Tretli S, Dahlback A, Moan J. Vitamin D3 from sunlight may improve the prognosis of breast-, colon- and prostate cancer (Norway). *Cancer Causes Control* 2004;15:149–58.

Rollier A. *Le Pansement Solaire.* Paris, Payot & Co. 1916.

Rostand RG. Ultraviolet light may contribute to geographic and racial blood pressure differences. *Hypertension* 1997;2(1):150–56.

Rowe PM. Why is rickets resurgent in the USA? *Lancet* 2001;357(9262):1100.

Sato Y, Metoki N, Iwamoto J, Satoh K. Amelioration of osteoporosis and hypovitaminosis D by sunlight exposure in stroke patients. *Neurology* 2003;61(3):338–342.

Scott BO. The history of ultraviolet therapy. In Licht S (ed.) *Therapeutic Electricity and Ultraviolet Radiation.* Physical Medicine Library Vol 4. Elizabeth Licht. Connecticut.1967. p196.

Scragg R, Khaw KT, Murphy S. Effect of winter oral vitamin D3 supplementation on cardiovascular risk factors in elderly adults. *Eur J Clin Nutr* 1995;49:640–46.

Soranus of Ephesus. *Soranus' Gynæcology.* (trans. O Temkin) Baltimore, Johns Hopkins University Press 1991.

Spencer FA et al. Seasonal distribution of acute myocardial infarction in the second national registry of myocardial infarction. *J Am Coll Cardiol* 1998;31:1226–33.

Sullivan SS et al. Adolescent girls in Maine are at risk for vitamin D insufficiency *J Am Diet Assoc* 2005;105:971–74.

The EURODIAB substudy 2 study group. Vitamin D supplement in early childhood and risk for type 1 (insulin dependent) diabetes mellitus. *Diabetalogica* 1999;42(1):51–54.

Trivedi DP, Doll R, and Khaw KT. Effect of four monthly oral vitamin D3 (cholecalciferol) supplementation on fractures and mortality in men and women living in the community: randomised double blind controlled trial. *BMJ* 2003;326:469.

Tuohimaa P, Tenkanen L, Ahonen M et al. Both high and low levels of blood vitamin D are associated with a higher prostate cancer risk: a longitudinal, nested case-control study in the Nordic countries. *Int J Cancer* 2004;108:104–08.

Van Amerongen BM, Dijkstra CD, Lips P, Polman CH. Multiple sclerosis and vitamin D: an update. *Euro J Clin Res* 2004;58:1095–1109.

Van der Mei IAF et al. Past exposure to sun, skin phenotype, and risk of multiple sclerosis: case-control study *BMJ* 2003;327:316.

Van der Vielen RPJ et al. Serum vitamin D concentrations among elderly people in Europe. *Lancet* 1995;346:207–10.

Van Veldhuizen PJ, Taylor SA, Williamson S, Drees BM. Treatment of vitamin D deficiency in patients with metastatic prostate cancer may improve bone pain and muscle strength. *J Urol* 2000;163:187–190.

Veith R and Fraser D. Vitamin D insufficiency: no recommended dietary allowance exists for this nutrient. *Can Med Assoc J* 2002;166(12):1541–42.

Veith R, Cole DE, Hawker GA et al. Wintertime vitamin D insufficiency is common in young Canadian women, and their vitamin D intake does not prevent it. *Eur J Clin Nutr* 2001;55:1091–97.

Veith R, Kimball S. Vitamin D in congestive heart failure. *Am J Clin Nutr* 2006;83:731–32.

Vieth R. Vitamin D supplementation, 25-hydroxyvitamin D concentrations, and safety. *Am J Clin Nutr* 1999;69:842–56.

Vieth R. Why the optimal requirement for vitamin D3 is probably much higher than what is officially recommended for adults. *J Steroid Biochem Mol Biol* 2004;89–90: 575–79.

Watson KE, Abrolat ML, Malone LL et al. Active serum vitamin D levels are inversely correlated with coronary calcification. *Circulation* 1997;96:1755–60.

Welch TR. Vitamin D-deficient rickets: the reemergence of a once-conquered disease. *J Pediatr* 2000;137:143–45.

Wharton B and Bishop N. Rickets. *Lancet* 2003;362:1389–1400.

Williams HC. Melanoma with no sun exposure. *Lancet* 1995;346:581.

Working Group of the Australian and New Zealand Bone and Mineral Society, Endocrine Society of Australia and Osteoporosis Australia. Vitamin D and adult bone health in Australia and New Zealand: a position statement. *Med J Aust* 2005 Mar 21;182(6):281–5.

Zhou W, Suk R, Liu G et al. Vitamin D is associated with improved survival in early stage non-small cell lung cancer patients. *Cancer Epidemiol Biomarkers Prev* 2005;14:2303–09.

Zimmet P, Alberti KG, Shaw J. Global and societal implications of the diabetes epidemic. *Nature* 2001 Dec 13;414(6865):782–7.

Zitterman A et al. Low vitamin D status: a contributing factor in the pathogenesis of congestive heart failure. *J Am Coll Cardiology* 2003;43:105–112.

Zitterman A. Vitamin D in preventive medicine: are we ignoring the evidence? *Brit J Nutr* 2003;89:552–72.

Zittermann A, Schleithoff SS, Koerfer R. Putting cardiovascular disease and vitamin D insufficiency into perspective. *Br J Nutr* 2005;94(4):483–92.

Zlotkin S. Vitamin D concentrations in Asian children living in England. Limited vitamin D intake and use of sunscreens may lead to rickets. *BMJ* 1999;318(7195):1417.

Chapter 5. Superbugs and the Sun

Acra A et al. Sunlight as disinfectant. *Lancet* 1989 Feb 4;280.

Alanis AJ. Resistance to antibiotics: are we in the post-antibiotic era? *Arch Med Res* 2005 Nov–Dec;36(6):697–705.

Anon. Annotations – natural and artificial sun cure in tuberculosis of the lungs. *Lancet* 1923 4th August:237–238.

Appelbaum PC. MRSA – the tip of the iceberg. *Clin Microbiol Infect* 2006 Apr;12 Suppl 2:3–10.

Bauer TM et al. An epidemiological study assessing the relative importance of airborne and direct contact transmission of microorganisms in a medical intensive care unit. *J Hosp Infect* 1990;15(4):301–309.

Beggs C. Ultraviolet light sterilisation of air. Proc Int Conference on Indoor Air Biocontaminants: Health Effects and Prevention. Intl Soc Built Environment, Dijon, France, 2001. p162–178.

Beggs CB. The airborne transmission of infection in hospital buildings: fact or fiction? *Ind Built Environ* 2003;12(1–2):9–18.

Bodington G. *An Essay on the Treatment and Cure of Pulmonary Consumption, On Principles N, Rational and Successful.* Longmans 1840. Reprinted London, The New Sydenham Society 1901.

Brock AJ. *Greek Medicine: Being Extracts Illustrative of Medical Writers from Hippocrates to Galen.* Library of Greek Thought. London, JM Dent, 1929.

Buchbinder L. et al. Studies on microorganisms in simulated room Environments III. The survival rates in streptococci in the presence of natural daylight, sunlight and artificial illumination. *J Bacteriol* 1941;42(3):353–366.

Buchbinder L et al. Studies on microorganisms in simulated room environments VII. Further observations on the survival rates of streptococci and pneumococci in daylight and Darkness. *J Bacteriol* 1942;42(5):545–555.

Buchbinder L. The bactericidal effects of daylight and sunlight on chained gram positive cocci in simulated room environment: theoretical and practical considerations. In *Aerobiology*, (ed. FR Moulton), Amer Assoc Adv Sci. Washington, Smithsonian Institute 1942, p267–270.

Buchbinder L. The transmission of certain infections of respiratory origin. *J American Med Assoc* 1942 Feb 28;718–730.

Cook GC. Early use of 'open-air' treatment for 'pulmonary phthisis' at the Dreadnought Hospital, Greenwich, 1900–1905. *Postgrad Med* 1999 Jun;75(884):326–7.

Cooper BS, Medley GF, Stone SP, Kibbler CC et al. Methicillin-resistant Staphylococcus aureus in hospitals and the community: stealth dynamics and control catastrophes. *Proc Natl Acad Sci USA.* 2004 Jul 6;101(27):10223–28.

Dowell SF. Seasonal variation in host susceptibility and cycles of certain infectious diseases. *Emerg Infect Dis* 2001;7:369–74.

Dowell SF et al. Seasonal patterns of invasive pneumococcal disease. *Emerg Infect Dis* 2003 May; 9(5): 573–579.

Dowell SF, Ho MS. Seasonality of infectious diseases and severe acute respiratory syndrome-what we don't know can hurt us. *Lancet Infect Dis* 2004 Nov;4(11):704–8.

Downes A, Blunt TP. Researches on the effect of light upon bacteria and other organisms. *Proc Roy Soc* 1877;26:488–500.

Duckworth G. Controlling methicillin resistant Staphylococcus aureus. Time to return to more stringent methods of control in the United Kingdom? *BMJ* 2003;327:1177–78.

Drews TD, Temte JL, Fox BC. Community-associated methicillin-resistant Staphylococcus aureus: review of an emerging public health concern. *WMJ* 2006 Jan;105(1):52–7.

Fairclough SJ. Why tackling MRSA needs a comprehensive approach. *Br J Nurs* 2006 Jan 26–Feb 8;15(2):72–5.

Garrod LP. Some observations on hospital dust with special reference to light as a hygienic safeguard. *BMJ* 1944 Feb 19th; 245–257.

Griffith F. Epidemics in Schools. Medical Research Council Special Report. No. 227 London, HMSO 1938.

Grundmann H et al. Emergence and resurgence of meticillin-resistant Staphylococcus aureus as a public-health threat. *Lancet* 2006 Sep;368(9538):874–85.

Hill L.E. *Sunshine and Open-Air: Their Influence on Health with Special Reference to Alpine Climates.* London, Edward Arnold and Co., Second Edition, 1925.

Hill LE, Campell A. *Health and Environment.* London, Edward Arnold and Co. 1925.

Holme C. Tuberculosis: story of medical failure. *BMJ* 1998;317:1260.

Hope-Simpson RE. Sunspots and flu: a correlation. *Nature* 1978;275:86.

Hope-Simpson RE. The role of season in the epidemiology of influenza. *J Hyg* 1981 Feb;86(1):35–47.

House of Commons Committee of Public Accounts. Twenty fourth Report of Session 2004–05. Improving Patient Care by Reducing the Risk of Hospital Acquired Infection: a Progress Report. London, HMSO 2005.

House of Lords. Resistance to Antibiotics and other Antimicrobial Agents. House of Lords Science and Technology Committee 7th Report, London, HMSO 1998.

Hoyle F, Wickramasinghe NC. Sunspots and Influenza. *Nature* 1990 Jan 25; 343:304.

Hoyle F, Wickramasinghe C. The dilemma of influenza. *Curr Sci* 2000 May 10;78(9):1057–58.

Huber JB. Civilization and tuberculosis. Brit J Tuberculosis 1907;1:156-159.

Hudson, B, Hill LE. Some clinical observations on heliotherapy in pulmonary tuberculosis. *Lancet* 1924 June 7:1147.

Jeyaratnam D, Reid C, Kearns A, Klein J. Community associated MRSA: an alert to paediatricians. *Arch Dis Child* 2006 Jun;91(6):511–2.

Keep PJ: Stimulus deprivation in windowless rooms. *Anaesthesia* 1977;32:598–602

Kisacky JS. Restructuring isolation: hospital architecture, medicine, and disease prevention. *Bull Hist Med* 2005; 79(1)1–49.

Kollef MH, Micek ST. Methicillin-resistant Staphylococcus aureus: a new community-acquired pathogen? *Curr Opin Infect Dis* 2006 Apr;19(2):161–8.

Larkin, ML. Intensive care delirium: the effect of outside deprivation in a windowless unit. *Arch Intern Med* 1972 Aug;225.

Lonnen J et al. Solar and photocatalytic disinfection of protozoan, fungal and bacterial microbes in drinking water. *Water Res* 2005 Mar;39(5):877–83.

Ne'eman E, Craddock J, Hopkinson RG. Sunlight requirements in buildings -I. social survey. *Build and Environ* 1976;11:217–238.

NHS. Infection Control in the Built Environment: Design and Planning. London, NHS Estates 2001.

Nightingale F. *Notes on Hospitals.* 3rd Edition, London, Longman, Roberts and Green, 1863.

Nightingale F. *Notes on Nursing; What it is and What it is Not.* New York, Dover Publications 1969.

Oates PM, Shanahan P, Polz MF.Solar disinfection (SODIS): simulation of solar radiation for global assessment and application for point-of-use water treatment in Haiti. *Water Res* 2003 Jan;37(1):47–54.

Ormerod LP. Multidrug-resistant tuberculosis (MDR-TB): epidemiology, prevention and treatment. *Br Med Bull* 2005 Jun 14;73–74:17–24.

Ownby H, Frederick J, Mortensen R, Ownby D, Russo J. Seasonal variations in tumor size at diagnosis and immunological responses in human breast cancer. *Invasion Metastasis* 1986;6:246–56.

Parasad, GV, Nash MM, Zaltman JS. Seasonal variation in outpatient blood pressure in stable renal transplant recipient. *Transplantation* 2001;72(11):1792–1794.

Plowman RM, Graves N, Roberts JA. *Hospital Acquired Infection.* London, Office of Health Economics 1997.

Ransome A, Delephine, S. On the influence of natural agents on the virulence of the tubercle bacillus. *Proc Roy Soc* 1894;56:51–56.

Ransome A. *The Principles of 'Open-air' Treatment of Phthisis and of Sanatorium Construction.* London, Smith Elder & Co. 1903.

Raviglione MC, Snider DE Jr, Kochi A. Global epidemiology of tuberculosis. Morbidity and mortality of a worldwide epidemic. *JAMA* 1995 Jan 18;273(3):220–6.

Rose A et al. Solar disinfection of water for diarrhoeal prevention in southern India. *Arch Dis Child* 2006;91:139–141.

Scott F. Dowell, Pell J, Cobbe S. Seasonal variations in coronary heart disease. *QJM* 1999;92:689–96.

Smith CR. Survival of tubercule bacilli. *Am Rev Tuberculosis* 1942;45(3):334–345.

Stevens FA. The bactericidal properties of UV irradiated lipids of the skin. *Exp Med* 1937;65:121.

Ulrich R: Effects of interior design on wellness: Theory and recent scientific research. *J Health Care Interior Design* 1990;102–103.

Ulrich RS, Zimring C, Quan X, Joseph A. The Role of the Physical Environment in the Hospital of the 21st Century. The Center for Health Design, 2004. (www.healthdesign.org/research/reports/physical_environ.php).

Watts GT. Ultraviolet light for sterilisation. *Lancet* 1987 Oct 15;912.

Webby RJ, Webster RG. Are we ready for pandemic influenza? *Science* 2003 Nov 28;302(5650):1519–22.

Weinstein L. Editorial: Influenza-1918, a revisit? *N Engl J Med* 1976 May 6;294(19):1058–60.

Chapter 6. Overcoming Light Deprivation

Aeschylus. *Prometheus Bound and Other Plays.* (trans. P Vellacott) London, Penguin, 1961.

Anon. *One Man's Vision: The Story of Joseph Rowntree Village Trust.* London, Allen and Unwin, 1954.

Anon. *The Bournville Village Trust 1900–1955.* Birmingham, Bournville Village Trust, 1956.

Atkinson W. The orientation of buildings and of streets in relation to sunlight. *Tech Quarterly* 1905 8th Sept;204–227.

Atkinson W. *The Orientation of Buildings or Planning for Sunlight.* New York, J Wiley & Sons, 1912.

Bernhard O. *Sonnenlichtbehandlung in der Chirurgie,* Stuttgart, Verlag von Ferdinand Enke, 1923.

Bernhard O. The need for climatic sanatoria for indigent patients suffering from surgical tuberculosis. *J State Med* 1931;39:333–345.

Burnett J. *A Social History of Housing.* University Press, Cambridge, 1980.

Bushnell H. *City Plans, in Work and Play; Or Literary Varieties.* London, Alex. Strahan & Co. 1864.

Cadbury G. The Bournville Estate – Objects of the Undertaking. Birmingham, Bournville Village Trust, Undated.

Cadbury G. *Town Planning.* London, Longmans Green and Co. 1915.

Campanella T. *The City of the Sun 1602* (trans. DJ Donno) Berkley, University of California Press, 1981.

Carey J. (ed.) *The Faber Book of Utopias.* London, Faber and Faber, 1999.

Cassedy JH. Hygeia: a mid-victorian dream of a city of health. *J Hist Med* 1962;17:217–228.

Conrads, U. *Programs and Manifestoes on 20th-Century Architecture.* Cambridge, M.I.T. Press, 1971.

Cowie LW. *A Dictionary of British Social History.* London, Bell and Sons Ltd London, 1973.

Eaton R. *Ideal Cities: Utopianism and the (Un)Built Environment.* London, Thames & Hudson, 2002.

Findlay L et al. A Study of Social and Economic Factors in the Causation of Rickets. Medical Research Committee Special Report 20. London, Galston and Sons 1918.

Finsen, NR. The red light treatment of small-pox, *BMJ* 1895 Dec 7;1412–1414.

Finsen, NR. *Phototherapy* (trans. JH Sequeira) London, Edward Arnold, 1901.

Finsen NR. The red light treatment of small-pox: a reply. *Lancet* 1904 Nov 5;1272.

Galton, D. *Healthy Hospitals.* Oxford, Clarendon Press, 1893.

Gauvain HJ. The sun cure – ailing children's new hope. *The Times* 1922 11th May:17–18.

George WL. *Labour and Housing at Port Sunlight.* London, Alston Rivers Ltd, 1909.

Henderson HE. John of Gaddesden, variola and the Finsen-light cure. *Cleveland Medical Journal* 1904 Oct;436–441.

Henderson DA et al. Smallpox as a biological weapon, in *Bioterrorism: Guidelines for Medical and Public Health Management.* (eds. DA Henderson, TV Inglesby, T O'Toole), Chicago, *JAMA* and Archived Journals, 2002, pp99–120.

Howard E. *Garden Cities of To-Morrow.* London, Swann Sonnenschein, 1902.

Johnson BG et al. Buildings and Health – indoor climate and effective energy use, Swedish Council for Building Research, Stockholm, Sweden, 1991.

Knibbs GH. The theory of city design. *J and Proc Roy Soc New South Wales* 1901; 35:62–112.

Latham A, West AW. *The Prize Essay on the Creation of a Sanatorium for the Treatment of Tuberculosis in England.* London, Balleri.

Lever WH. Land for Houses. Paper read before North End Liberal Club [Birkenhead], Tuesday 4th October 1898, p 5, quoted in E Hubbard, M Shippobolton. A Guide to Port Sunlight Village. Liverpool University Press 1990.

Mayer E. *Sunlight and Artificial Radiation.* London, Balliere, Tindall and Cox 1926.

Mumford L. *The Culture of Cities.* London, Secker and Warburg 1938.

Nobel Lectures, *Physiology or Medicine 1901–1921,* Elsevier Publishing Company, Amsterdam, 1967

Olbert, Th. *Lancet* 1962 April 7;746.

Page JK. (Ed.), Indoor Environment: Health Aspects of Air Quality, Thermal Environment, Light and Noise, WHO/EHE/RUD/90.2, World Health Organization, Geneva, 1990.

Parker B, Urwin R. *The Art of Building a Home.* London, Longman Green & Co. 1901.

Potter J. The history of the disease called lupus. *Hist Med Allied Sci* 1993;48:80–90.

Pugh WTG. *Practical Nursing.* London, William Blackwood and Sons Ltd. 1953.

Purdom CB. *The Garden City, a Study in the Development of a Modern Town.* London, Dent and Sons MCMXIII.

Redford DB. *Akhenaten: The Heretic King.* Princeton, Princeton University Press 1987.

RIBA. The Orientation of Buildings – Being the Report of the RIBA Joint Committee on the Orientation of Buildings. London, Royal Institute of British Architects 1933.

Ricketts TF, Byles JB. Further note on the red light treatment of small-pox. *Lancet* 1904 Nov 26;1490–1491.

Ricketts TF, Byles JB. Red light treatment of small-pox. *Lancet* 1904 July 30;287–290.

Rollier A. *La Cure de Soleil.* Lausanne, Payot 1916.

Rollier A. *Quarante Ans d'Héliothérapie.* Lausanne, University of Lausanne 1944.

Rollier A. The construction of an institution for the heliotherapeutic treatment of surgical tuberculosis. *Tubercle* 1921 March;241–250.

Rollier A. The share of the sun in the prevention and treatment of tuberculosis. *BMJ* 1922 Oct 21st; 741–745.

Rollier A. Tuberculosis finds cure in the Leysin heliotherapy clinics. *The Modern Hospital* 1923;21(3):255–260.

Rollier, A. *Heliotherapy – with Special Consideration of Surgical Tuberculosis.* 1st Edition, London, Oxford Medical Publications 1923.

Saleeby CW. *Sunlight and Health.* London, Nisbet and Co. 1929.

Smith FB. *The Retreat of Tuberculosis 1850–1950.* London, Croom Helm 1988.

Sourkes TL. *Nobel Prizewinners in Medicine 1901–1965.* New York, Abelard-Schuman 1966.

Stein J. Bringing architecture to light: the pioneering work of William Atkinson. http://www.wit.edu/Academics/HSSM/context/vol1/stein.html

Van der Leun JC, de Gruijl FR. Influences of ozone depletion on human and animal health, Chapter 4 in *UV-B Radiation and Ozone Depletion: Effects on Humans, Animals, Plants, Microorganisms, and Materials.* (ed. M Tevini) Ann Arbor: Lewis Publishers 1993.

Venolia C. Health, buildings and the sun. *SunWorld* 1988;12(2):48–51.

Ward Richardson B. *Hygeia, a City of Health.* London, Macmillan 1876.

Chapter 7. Temples to the Sun

Anon. Living with Le Corbusier: Unité d'Habitation, Marseille. *Prog Arch* 1970 Nov;90–95.

Anon. Marseille: a housing consultant's look at Le Corbusier's Unité d'Habitation after two decades of use. *Arch Plus* 1974 Jan/Feb;2(1):86–91.

Anon. Mies' miraculous survivor; Architects: Ludwig Mies van der Rohe. *Arch Rev* 1993 Apr;92,(1154):74–79.

Anon. Proportion and beauty – the Lovell Beach House by Rudolph Michael Schindler, Newport Beach, 1922–1926. *Soc Arch Hist J* 1986 Dec;45:374–388.

Anon. Rudolf Schindler, 1887–1953: the least appreciated. Illustrated by 3 projects. (1), Lovell Beach House, Newport Beach, Los Angeles. (2), Schindler's house and office, King's Road, Hollywood, Los Angeles. (3), Kallis house and studio, Los Angeles. *AJ* 1969 Feb 19;476–479.

Anon. Sun House, Frognal Way, Hampstead, London, designed (1935) by E. Maxwell Fry. *AJ* 1936 Aug 13;210–214.

Atkinson W. The orientation of buildings and of streets in relation to sunlight. *Tech Quarterly* 1905 8th Sept;204–227.

Atkinson W. *The Orientation of Buildings or Planning for Sunlight.* New York, J Wiley & Sons, 1912.

Butti K.Perlin JK. *A Golden Thread – 2500 Years of Solar Architecture and Technology.* London, Marion Boyars, 1980.

Campbell M. From cure chair to chaise longue: medical treatment and the form of the modern recliner. *J Design Hist* 1999;12(4)327–343.

Campbell M. What tuberculosis did for modernism: the influence of a curative environment on modernist design and architecture. *Med Hist* 2005 October 1;49(4):463–488.

Carey J. (ed.) *The Faber Book of Utopias.* London, Faber and Faber, 1999.

Conrads U. *Program and Manifestoes on 20th-Century Architecture.* Cambridge, M.I.T. Press, 1971.

Curtis, WJR. *Modern Architecture Since 1900.* 3rd ed. Oxford, Phaidon Press Ltd, 1992.

Dunster D. *Key buildings of the twentieth century. Vol. 1: Houses 1900–1944.* London, Architectural Press, 1985.

Eaton R. *Ideal Cities: Utopianism and the (Un)Built Environment.* London, Thames & Hudson, 2002.

Frampton, Kenneth. *Modern Architecture, A Critical History.* 3rd ed. London: Thames and Hudson, 1992.

Frampton K. *Le Corbusier.* London, Thames and Hudson, 2001.

Fry M. *Fine Building.* London, Faber and Faber Ltd, 1944.

Giedion S. *Mechanisation Takes Command.* Oxford University Press, 1948.

Glancey J. *Twentieth Century Architecture.* London, Carlton Books, 2000.

Gold J. Creating the Charter of Athens: CIAM and the functional city, 1933–43. *Town Planning Rev* 1998 July;69(3):225–248.

Hines TS. *Richard Neutra and the Search for Modern Architecture.* New York, Oxford University Press, 1982.

Howard A. Developing a lifestyle: the design and building of Max Fry's Sun House, Hampstead, and Connell Ward & Lucas' house at 66 Frognal, also in Hampstead; Architect: Trevor Dannat. *Building Design* 1976 Oct;320:20–21.

J.M. Richards. *800 Years of Finnish Architecture.* Vancouver: David and Charles, 1978.

Lamprecht B. *Richard Neutra.* London, Taschen 2004.

Le Corbusier, *The Marseille Block.* (trans. G Sainsbury), London, The Harville Press, London 1953.

Le Corbusier. *La Ville Radieuse.* Paris, Vincent, Fréal, 1933.

Le Corbusier. *Towards a New Architecture.* London, John Rodker 1931.

Lloyd Wright F. *The Natural House.* New York, Horizon Press 1954.

Moos S. *Le Corbusier: Elements of a Style.* Cambridge, MIT Press 1979.

Mumford L. Machines for living. *Fortune* 1933 Feb;VII:78–80.

Murphy KD. The Villa Savoye and the modernist historic monument. *J Society of Arch Historians* 2002 Mar;61(1):68–89.

Nuttgens P. *Understanding Modern Architecture.* London, Unwin Hyman 1988.

Page JK. (ed.) Indoor Environment: Health Aspects of Air Quality, Thermal Environment, Light and Noise. WHO/EHE/RUD/90.2, World Health Organization, Geneva, 1990.

Pevsner N. *The Sources of Modern Architecture and Design.* London, Thames and Hudson 1975.

Porteous C. *The New Eco-Architecture Alternatives from the Modern Movement.* London, Spon Press 2002.

Powers A. Villa Savoye, Ile-de-France; Architect (1928): Le Corbusier. *Country Life* 1994 July 7;188(27):74–77.

Rollier A. The share of the sun in the prevention and treatment of tuberculosis. *BMJ* 1922 Oct 21; 741–745.

Rollier A. Tuberculosis finds cure in the Leysin heliotherapy clinics. *The Modern Hospital* 1923;21(3):255–260.

Rollier A. *Heliotherapy – with Special Consideration of Surgical Tuberculosis.* 1st Edition, London, Oxford Medical Publications 1923.

Sbriglio J. *Le Corbusier: La Villa Savoye.* Paris, Fondation Le Corbusier 1999.

Sedy V, Sapak J. Villa Tugendhat, Brno (1928–1930); Architects: Ludwig Mies van der Rohe. *Domus* 1986 Dec;678:25–37.

Sharp D. *Sources of Modern Architecture.* London, Granada Publishing 1981.

Smith PF. *Architecture and the Human Dimension.* London, George Goodwin Ltd 1979.

Stein J. Bringing architecture to light: the pioneering work of William Atkinson. http://www.wit.edu/Academics/HSSM/context/vol1/stein.html

Walker FA. Tugendhat house – what shall be its future; Architects: Ludwig Mies van der Rohe. *RIBA J* 1978 Feb;85(2):60–61.

Wander A. Tuberculosis sanatoria: at Paimio, Finland; Architect: A. Aalto; at Montana, Switzerland *AJ* 1933 Oct 5; 420–423.

Weston R. *Key Buildings of the Twentieth Century: Plans, Sections and Elevations.* New York, WW Norton 2004.

Whittick A. *European Architecture in the Twentieth Century.* Aylesbury, Leonard Hill Books 1974.

Wiebensen D. *Tony Garnier, The Cite Industrielle.* London, Studio Vista 1969.

Worpole K. *Here Comes the Sun: Architecture and Public Space in Twentieth-Century European Culture.* London, Reaktion Books 2000.

Chapter 8. Making the Most of Light

Aschoff J et al. Lifetime of flies under influence of time displacement. *Naturwissenschaften* 1971;58:574 (In German).

Atkinson W. The orientation of buildings and of streets in relation to sunlight. *Tech Quarterly* 1905 8th Sept; 204–227.

Baker N, Steemers K. *Daylight Design of Buildings: A Handbook for Architects and Engineers.* London, James & James Ltd, 2001.

Bataille V et al. A multicentre epidemiological study on sunbed use and cutaneous melanoma in Europe. *Eur J Cancer* 2005 Sep;41(14):2141–9.

Bataille V et al. Exposure to the sun and sunbeds and the risk of cutaneous melanoma in the UK: a case-control study. *Eur J Cancer* 2004. Feb;40(3):429–35.

Beral V, et al. Malignant melanoma and exposure to fluorescent lighting at work. *Lancet* 1982;ii:290–293.

Berwick M. et al. Sun exposure and mortality from melanoma. *J Nat Cancer Inst* 2005 February 2;97;3:195–198

Booker JM, Roseman C. A seasonal pattern of hospital medication errors in Alaska. *Psychiatry Res* 1995 Aug 28;57(3):251–7.

Boubekri M, Hulliv RB, Boyer LL. Impact of window size and sunlight penetration on office workers' mood and satisfaction: a novel way of assessing sunlight. *Environ and Behav* 1991;23(4), 474–493.

Boubekri M. An argument for daylighting legislation because of health. *J Human-Environ System* 2004;7(2):51–56.

Boubekri M. An overview of current daylighting legislation. *J. Human-Environ System* 2004;7(2):58–63.

Boubekri, M. On the issue of illuminance requirement as a design criterion. *J Human-Environment System* 1999;3(1):71–76.

Brainard GC and Hanafin JP. The effects of light on human health and behaviour: relevance to architectural lighting. Proc CIE Expert Symposium Light and Health: Non-visual Effects, Vienna, Austria, 30 September–2 October, 2004. p 2–9.

Brown GZ, DeKay M. *Sun, Wind & Light: Architectural Design Strategies.* New York, John Wiley & Sons, 2000.

Buchanan TL, Barker KN, Gibson JT, Jiang BC, Pearson RE. Illumination and errors in dispensing. *Am J Hosp Pharm* 1991;48(10):2137–2145.

Butti K. Perlin JK. *A Golden Thread – 2500 Years of Solar Architecture and Technology.* London, Marion Boyars, 1980.

Chel VGM et al. Ultraviolet irradiation corrects vitamin D3 deficiency and suppresses secondary hyperparathyroidism in the elderly, *J Bone Mineral Res* 1998;13(8):1238–1242.

CIBSE. Daylighting and Window Design. CIBSE Lighting Guide LG10, Chartered Institution of Building Services Engineers, London, 1999.

Czeisler CA et al. Bright light resets the human circadian pacemaker independent of the timing of the sleep-wake cycle. *Science* 1986;233:667–671.

Czeisler CA et al. Exposure to bright light and darkness to treat physiologic maladaptation to night work. *N Engl J Med* 1990;322:1253–1259.

Di Lorenzo L et al. Effect of shift work on body mass index: results of a study performed in 319 glucose-tolerant men working in a Southern Italian industry. *Int J Obes Relat Metab Disord* 2003 Nov;27(11):1353–8.

Dumont M. Exposure to the light-dark cycle in day and night workers. Proc CIE Expert Symposium Light and Health: Non-visual Effects, Vienna, Austria, 30 September–2 October, 2004. p107–110.

Eastman CI et al. Light treatment for sleep disorders: consensus report. VI. shift work. *J Biol Rhythms* 1995;10:157–164.

Evans GW, McCoy JM. When buildings don't work: the role of architecture in human health. *Env Pschy* 1998;18:85–94.

Fitzpatrick M. *The Tyranny of Health: Doctors and the Regulation of Lifestyle.* London, Routledge, 2001.

Gangwisch JE, Malaspina D, Boden-Albala B, Heymsfield SB. Inadequate sleep as a risk factor for obesity: analyses of the NHANES I. *Sleep.* 2005 Oct 1;28(10):1289–96.

Grant WB, Holick MF. Benefits and requirements of vitamin D for optimal health: a review. *Altern Med Rev* 2005;10:94–111.

Gropius W. *Scope of Total Architecture.* London, Allen and Unwin Ltd. 1956.

Hayward RA et al. Estimating hospital deaths due to medical errors: preventability is in the eye of the reviewer *JAMA* 2001;286:415–420.

Holick FM. Vitamin D: A millennium perspective. *J Cell Biochem* 2003;88:296–307.

Hollis B. Editorial: The determination of circulating 25-hydroxyvitamin D: no easy task. *J Clin End and Metab* 2004; 89: 3149–3151.

Ishizaki M et al. The influence of work characteristics on body mass index and waist to hip ratio in Japanese employees. *Ind Health* 2004 Jan;42(1):41–9.

King K, Negus K, Vance JC. Heat stress in motor vehicles: a problem in infancy. *Pediatrics* 1981;68:579–582.

Lam WMC. *Sunlighting as Formgiver for Architecture.* New York, Van Nostrand Reinhold Co, 1986.

Lim HW et al. Sunlight, tanning booths, and vitamin D. *J Am Acad Dermatol* 2005;52:868–76.

Leather P et al. Windows in the workplace: sunlight, view and occupant stress. *Environ and Behav* 1998 Nov;6:739–762.

McColl SL, Veitch JA. Full-spectrum fluorescent lighting: A review of its effects on physiology and health. *Psychol Med* 2001;31:949–964.

McLaren C, Null J, Quinn J. Heat stress from enclosed vehicles: moderate ambient temperatures cause significant temperature rise in enclosed vehicles. *Pediatrics* 2005;116;109–112.

McNicholl A, Lewis O. Daylighting Buildings The European Commission Directorate-General for Energy (DGXVII) Energy Research Group. University College, Dublin 1994.

Miller N, McGowan T. How will light and health research affect electric lighting and lighting design? Proc CIE Expert Symposium Light and Health: Non-visual Effects, Vienna, Austria, 30 September–2 October, 2004. p137–41.

Nagaya T, Yoshida H, Takahashi H, Kawai M. Markers of insulin resistance in day and shift workers aged 30–59 years. *Int Arch Occup Environ Health* 2002 Oct;75(8):562–8.

Neale VC, Woloshynowych M. Adverse events in British hospitals: preliminary retrospective record review. *BMJ* 2001 March 3;322(7285):517–519.

Pauley SM. Lighting for the human circadian clock: recent research indicates that lighting has become a public health issue. *Med Hypoth* 2004;63:588–96.

Rea MS, Figueiro MG, Bullough, JD. Circadian photobiology: An emerging framework for lighting practice and research. *Ltg Res and Tech* 2002;34(3):177–190.

Rigel DS, et al. Relationship of fluorescent lights to malignant melanoma: Another view. *J Dermatol Surg Oncol* 1983;9:836–838.

Roberts KB, Roberts EC. The automobile and heat stress. *Pediatrics* 1976;58:101–104.

Samuels R. Solar efficient architecture and quality of life: the role of daylight and sunlight in ecological and psychological well-being. In, AAM Sayigh (ed.), Proc 1st World Renewable Energy Congress. Reading, UK, London, Pergamon Press 1990 p. 2653–2659.

Sato Y, Iwamoto J, Kanoko T, Satoh K. Low-dose vitamin D prevents muscular atrophy and reduces falls and hip fractures in women after stroke: a randomized controlled trial. *Cerebrovasc Dis.* 2005;20(3):187–92.

Schernhammer ES et al. Rotating night shifts and risk of breast cancer in women participating in the Nurses' Health Study. *J Natl Cancer Inst* 2001;93:1563–1568.

Seidell JC. Obesity, insulin resistance and diabetes – a worldwide epidemic. *Br J Nutr* 2000 Mar;83 Suppl 1:S5–8.

Stevens R G, Rea M S. Light in the built environment: potential role of circadian disruption in endocrine disruption and breast cancer. *Cancer Causes Control* 2001;12:279–287.

Stein J. Bringing architecture to light: the pioneering work of William Atkinson. http://www.wit.edu/Academics/HSSM/context/vol1/stein.html

Sudjic D. *The Edifice Complex : How the Rich and Powerful Shape the World.* London, Allen Lane, 2005.

Surpure JS. Heat-related illness and the automobile. *Ann Emerg Med* 1982 May;11(5):263–5 19

Taheri S, Lin L, Austin D, Young T, Mignot E. Short sleep duration is associated with reduced leptin, elevated ghrelin, and increased body mass index. *PLoS Med* 2004 Dec;1(3):e62.

Tangpricha V, Turner A et al. Tanning is associated with optimal vitamin D status (serum 25-hydroxyvitamin D concentration) and higher bone mineral density. *Am J Clin Nutr* 2004;80:1645–9.

Taylor D, Bruhns H. Maintenance of the Database of UK Passive Solar Buildings Final Report ETSU S/01/0261/REP. Energy Technology Support Unit Harwell, Oxford 1999.

Venning G. Recent developments in vitamin D deficiency and muscle weakness among elderly people. *BMJ* 2005 Mar 5;330(7490):524–6.

Veith R. Vitamin D supplementation, 25-hydroxyvitamin D and safety. *Am J Clin Nutr* 1999; 69: 842–56.

Vieth R. Why the optimal requirement for vitamin D3 is probably much higher than what is officially recommended for adults. *J Steroid Biochem and Mol Biol* 2004;89–90: 575–579.

Walter SD et al. The association of cutaneous malignant melanoma and fluorescent light exposure. *Am J Epidemiol* 1992;135:749–762.

Chapter 9. The Light Revolution

Boubekri M et al. Impact of window size and sunlight penetration on office workers' mood and satisfaction. *Environ and Behav* 1991;23(4):474–493.

Brainard GC and Hanafin JP. The effects of light on human health and behaviour: relevance to architectural lighting. Proc CIE Expert Symposium Light and Health: Non-visual Effects, Vienna, Austria, 30 September–2 October, 2004. pp 2–9.

BRE. EcoHomes 2005 – The environmental rating for homes. The Guidance – 2005 / Issue1.1. Building Research Establishment. Watford 2005.

BRE. EcoHomes 2005 – The environmental rating for homes. Developer Sheets – 2005 / Issue 1.1. Building Research Establishment. Watford 2005.

Brundage JF et al. Energy efficient buildings pose higher risk of respiratory infection: study. *J Am Med Assoc* 1998 Apr 8;259(14):2108–2112.

Cutler D Miller G. The role of public health improvements in health advances: the twentieth-century United States. *Demography* 2005;42(1)1–22.

DTI. Passive solar design: technology description. A sustainable energy technology route map on passive solar design. Department of Trade and Industry Renewable Energy Programme. http://www.ecdti.co.uk/CGIBIN/priamlnk.cgi?MP=CATSER%5EGINT65&CNO=1& CAT='EN12. 1st January 2003.

Fitzpatrick M, *The Tyranny of Health: Doctors and the Regulation of Lifestyle.* London: Routledge, 2001.

Freudenberg N. Time for a national agenda to improve the health of urban populations. *Am J Public Health* 2000;90:837–840.

Hill L.E. *Sunshine and Open-Air: Their Influence on Health with Special Reference to Alpine Climates.* London, Edward Arnold and Co., Second Edition, 1925.

Hill LE, Campell A. *Health and Environment.* London, Edward Arnold and Co. 1925.

LEED™ Green Building Rating System version 2.0. U.S. Green Building Council. Washington D.C. 2001.

Secretary of State for the Environment, Food and Rural Affairs. Climate Change The UK Programme 2006. Norwwich, HMSO 2006.

Taylor D, Bruhns H. Maintenance of the Database of UK Passive Solar Buildings Final Report ETSU S/01/0261/REP. Energy Technology Support Unit Harwell, Oxford 1999.

Further Reading

Boyce PR. *Human Factors in Lighting.* 2nd Edition. London, Taylor and Francis 2003.

Butti K. Perlin JK. *A Golden Thread – 2500 Years of Solar Architecture and Technology.* London, Marion Boyars 1980.

Downing D. *Day Light Robbery.* London, Arrow Books 1988.

Schuster S. *Sun and the Skin: Violation of Truth, in Panic Nation: Unpicking the Myths We're told about Food and Health.* (eds. S Feldman, V Marks), London, John Blake Publishing Ltd 2005.

Fitzpatrick M. *The Tyranny of Health: Doctors and the Regulation of Lifestyle.* London, Routledge 2001.

Foster R, Kreitzman L. *Rythms of Life: The Biological Clocks that Control the Daily Lives of Every Living Thing.* London, Profile Books Ltd 2004.

Gillie O. *Sunlight Robbery.* Health Research Forum Occasional Report No.1. London, Health Research Forum 2004.

Gillie O. *Sunlight, Vitamin D and Health.* Health Research Forum Occasional Report No.2. London, Health Research Forum 2006.

Holick MF, Jenkins M. *The UV Advantage.* New York, ibooks 2004.

Hyde PJ. *Sunlight, Vitamin D, and Prostate Cancer Risk.* Philadelphia, Xlibris 2002.

Kime ZR. *Sunlight Could Save Your Life.* California, World Health Publications 1980.

Liberman JI. *Light: Medicine of the Future.* Santa Fe, Bear & Co 1991.

Ott JN. *Health and Light.* New York, Pocket Books 1973.

Porteous C. *The New Eco-Architecture Alternatives from the Modern Movement.* London, Spon Press 2002.

Worpole K. *Here Comes the Sun: Architecture and Public Space in Twentieth-Century European Culture.* London, Reaktion Books 2000.

Index

Also by Richard Hobday

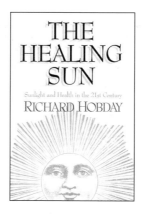

The Healing Sun
Sunlight and Health in the 21st Century
182 pages paperback with black & white photographs
ISBN 1-899171-97-5

The human race evolved under the sun, and for thousands of years lived in harmony with its heat and light. Yet over the last fifty years we have lost this close contact with the sun and its healing powers. We have become afraid of it.

However the sun is central to our well being and health. Did you know that:

- sunlight can help prevent and heal many common and often fatal diseases like breast cancer, heart disease, multiple sclerosis and osteoporosis
- before antibiotics, sunlight was used successfully to speed up the healing of wounds
- tanning moderately throughout the year is better than avoiding the sun altogether
- sudden bursts of strong solar radiation are unnatural and dangerous, protection needs to be built up slowly
- early morning sunlight in cool temperatures is particularly beneficial to the body
- prolonged exposure to artificial light puts the body under

great stress large numbers of people may be compromising their health through sunlight deficiency

- there is a substantial body of historical and contemporary evidence that suggests moderate sunbathing is far more beneficial than we are currently led to believe

The light and heat from the sun are indispensable to all nature. Humanity is also part of nature and needs sunlight for health and well being, for vitality and happiness. This book explains how and why we should welcome sunlight back into our lives safely! It shows how sunlight was used to prevent and cure diseases in the past, and how it can heal us and help us in the future.

available from your local bookstore
or directly from
www.findhornpress.com

Books, Card Sets, CDs & DVDs that inspire and uplift

For a complete catalogue,
please contact:

Findhorn Press Ltd
305a The Park, Findhorn
Forres IV36 3TE
Scotland, UK

Telephone
+44-(0)1309-690582
Fax
+44-(0)1309-690036
eMail
info@findhorpress.com

or consult our catalogue online
(with secure order facility) on

www.findhornpress.com